STEVE HALLIDAY

No Night Too Dark

HOW GOD TURNS DEFEAT INTO
GLORIOUS TRIUMPH

No Night Too Dark
© 1993 by Steve Halliday

Published by Multnomah Books
a part of the Questar Publishing Family

Edited by Larry R. Libby
Cover design by David Uttley
Artwork by Hilber Nelson

Printed in the United States of America

International Standard Book Number: 0-88070-560-4

Questar Publishers, Inc.
Post Office Box 1720
Sisters, Oregon 97759

93 94 95 96 97 98 99 00 01 02 — 10 9 8 7 6 5 4 3 2 1

Dedicated to
Rev. Wendell and Betty Boyer,
who provided me
with a breathtaking view
of the magnificence and grandeur of
God.

Contents

Acknowledgments

"Do not think of yourself more highly than you ought," the apostle Paul solemnly warned us, and I doubt there is an activity more suited to building deep humility than the creation of a book. I know that without the help of several talented and loyal friends, this book never would have blossomed beyond the germ of an idea. My profound thanks go out to several choice people:

To Pat Edmonds, Pat MaGee, and Ryan Wardell: Three courageous friends who agreed to critique the manuscript as it developed. The unfortunate author who grumbled, "For critics I care the five hundred thousandth part of the tythe of a half-farthing" obviously was not blessed with the sort of gentle opinions which helped to shape this manuscript.

To Ray Holder, Rob Shafar, and "Susan": The book would be much the poorer without the addition of your stories; thanks for your willingness to let me use them. I have no doubt that all three of you are well on your way to a shiny Oholiab!

To Liz Heaney: Editorial colleague, insightful reviewer, and cherished friend. You deserve a limerick:

> There once was a woman named Liz
> Who at editing books was a whiz.
> > Her judgment is keen,
> > Her manuscripts, lean.
> And for that, she's the best in the biz!

To Robin Georgioff: Perhaps Jawaharlal Nehru had your copyediting skills in mind when he said, "Obviously, the highest type of efficiency is that which can utilize existing material to the best advantage." It's amazing how even a single letter can make the difference between a good book and a goof one. Thanks!

To Don Jacobson: My guess is that this past year has taught you more about divine turnabouts that you care to know—maybe you should have written this book! You'll never know how much I appreciate you giving me a forum even when I decline an office.

To Larry Libby: The wag who said, "Diplomacy is the art of saying 'Nice Doggie' until you can find a stick" obviously never met you. Your gracious spirit, affirming words, editorial wisdom, and genuine humility define for me what "diplomacy" is all about. You don't get a limerick, but you, too, are clearly the "best in the biz." Alexander Pope spoke for me about you when he said, "Thou wert my guide, philosopher, and friend." *¡Dios te bendiga, Laurencio de las Palabras!*

Introduction

More than forty years ago a celebrated English churchman, Canon J. B. Phillips, wrote a little gem of a book titled, *Your God Is Too Small*. Phillips wrote the book after becoming alarmed that people had allowed the technology and pace of modern life to "shrink" God Almighty down to a more tolerable size. His book so challenged the Christian public that it is still in print.

If the good Canon were alive today, however, I don't think he'd write about a God who had become too small. The problem with the God of many people nowadays isn't that He's too small; it's that He's too weak.

Today's God is feeble. Pale. Doddering. Even anemic. People almost pity Him—the poor soul just can't seem to muster up the strength to properly run a universe as vast as this. No wonder He can't get a grip on the problems of our troubled little planet! That was Harold Kushner's basic conclusion in his runaway bestseller of a few years ago, *Why Bad Things Happen to Good People*. The fact that consumers bought the book by the truckload speaks volumes about our culture's vision of God. Had Phillips been alive to read Kushner's book, we might well have been blessed with a response from his pen titled, *Your God Is Too Frail*.

Now, I'm no J. B. Phillips, but since this eloquent man has gone on to his reward, I just can't let such a gargantuan blunder go unchallenged. I've seen God's mighty hand too many times to think for a moment that He's ready for retirement. And the startling thing is, I've seen that hand *in the very midst of what leads others to believe He's grown feeble.*

The surprising truth is that the Lord loves to take Satan's

best shots and deflect them straight back into his devilish midsection. He seems to delight in transforming what looks like a clear victory for Satan into a stunning triumph for God's people.

In fact—if I can say such a thing without getting into trouble—at times God almost acts, well, *puckish.* He not only brings good out of evil, He turns evil on its head. He not only overcomes the outrage, He turns it inside out. In mid-flight He mutates the Devil's deadliest bullets into Satan-seeking boomerangs. God will use the most unlikely scenarios to display His own omnipotence and the powerlessness of His enemies.

On television, in newspapers, and in "real life," all of us see more tragedy and heartache than we care to. We all have witnessed the devastating effects of both nature run amok and humankind gone savage.

But if you look closely and watch long enough, you will also witness something else, something incomparably precious...

You will see God at work.

And believe me, the God you will see is no weakling! Even in the midst of suffering and death and disease and worry and hunger and thirst and nakedness, you may see a sudden stab of light through the clouds...an inexplicable reversal of circumstances...a fragile flower of matchless beauty pushing its way through the rubble and devastation. Once you start looking for the distinctive fingerprints of God Almighty, this sometimes dark, sometimes turbulent life will never look the same. He is often exactly where you do not expect to see Him, bringing good out of bad, turning evil inside out. You might even say that *turnabout is God's play.*

This reminds me of a maxim popular several years ago. When someone quoted the phrase, "turnabout is fair play,"

10

it was another way of saying (as my friend, Ryan, is fond of reminding me whenever he thinks I'm about to spring a nasty surprise on him), "What goes around comes around."

I believe the saying also reflects a unique way God often operates in our world. Only I would amend it to say, "turnabout is *God's* play."

When our world is caving in, when things look as grim as they possibly can, when it seems as though Satan has applied the *coup de grace* to our fondest hopes and greatest desires—at precisely that point the Strong One steps in and brandishes the very evil for His glory.

This suggests even more than the glorious words of Romans 8:28: "And we know that in all things God works for the good of those who love him, who have been called according to his purpose." That wonderful text reminds us that God will use all of the events of our lives for our ultimate good. But God often goes beyond merely bringing good out of evil; frequently He uses *the very evil itself* to bless His people and bring glory to Himself.

The God I know and love and serve not only makes all things work together for the good of those who love Him, but sometimes He takes the very evil intended to destroy us and stands it on its head, so that even the evil itself works for our benefit and His glory.

Now, *that* is a God to worship! *That* is a God to adore!

And that is the God who fills the universe with His splendor—not some shuffling, half-dead, powerless deity who's in it way over His head.

In this book I frankly hope to prompt you to reconsider your God. I long for you to see Him for who He is, an unimaginably powerful and glorious God who loves His people with a furious and everlasting passion—even when those people are suffering.

I hope to accomplish this primarily by recounting for you stories of what God has done and is doing all around the globe. My goal is *not* to impress you with titillating accounts of thrilling adventures in remote and exotic locales, but to invite you to bask for awhile in the limitless goodness and love of God.

To *bask*. It has a nice sound, doesn't it? I learned a lot about basking years ago when I took my first commercial flight. It was in the dead of winter and some friends and I were flying from icy, frigid Minneapolis to balmy, sun-drenched Palm Springs. I'll never forget the shock when I stepped off the plane at the end of the flight. Just hours before I had fled the land of ten thousand (frozen) lakes. Chilled to the bone. Red-cheeked. Wrapped in layer upon layer of super-thermo-insulating, heavy-duty, glacierized tundrawear.

And then I stepped out...into Paradise.

Well, not quite Paradise. But at the time it was surely close enough. Seventy-eight sunny, cloudless, freckle-enhancing, golden degrees. Forget the mittens. Ditch the parkas. Pack away the long-johns and break out the suntan oil.

Glory!

That vacation, I learned to *bask*. To luxuriate in the warm, inviting rays of the California sun. I learned that my attitude skyrockets when I'm given the privilege to thaw my frozen extremities under bright skies and light, dry desert breezes. Basking does that for me...and my guess is that it would do the same for you. Whether we're talking about your body or your soul.

You may not live in the midwest, as I did at the time of my first Palm Springs trip. In fact, you may already call "home" some sunny spot such as southern California,

12

Florida, or Hawaii. But it may be you know all about being frozen. Your very soul seems stuffed into a devilish icebox, and you can't seem to prop open the door to escape. Life seems bitterly cold. Harsh. Unforgiving. And God seems very, very far away.

If that's how you feel, you've come to the right spot. Although I'm not a travel agent by trade, I would like to send you on a fabulous trip to bask in a place where bright skies and sub-tropical winds can thaw out the most frozen of souls. A place where icy blasts get turned into balmy breezes. Where snowdrifts blocking the door become sand dunes accenting the pool. Where crystalline icicles metamorphose into gurgling fountains and wind-chill factors into sun protection factors.

I'd like to send you to the land of divine turnabouts.

This sunny land has refreshed my own soul more than once. When the walls seemed to be closing in, when the wolf readied himself to lunge at my throat, when the darkness seemed about to choke out the light, divine travel agents have suddenly appeared at my side and transported me to God's fabulous Turnabout City.

Don't misunderstand. Physically I continued to occupy the same space; it was the landscape that miraculously changed. God took disastrous situations and transformed them into joyful celebrations. He changed hurtful blunders into eye-popping blessings and reversed frightful prospects into exhilarating realities.

Over the years I have learned that turnabout is God's play, and in the following pages I hope to show how this is as true today as it has been throughout history.

As you focus your attention on the everlasting God, you, too, may see your worst nightmares fade and vanish into the shadows as the astonishing brilliance of God's perfect plan for you takes shape. You, too, may be surprised at the unorthodox ways God chooses to bring Himself glory. But then again, it really shouldn't surprise us.

For if God really does specialize in turnabouts, as His Word claims, there truly can be *No Night Too Dark.*

Chapter 1

You Just Have to Laugh

*I*magine that you are stranded at a ranger station in the wilds of Kenya. Imagine further that it is the dead of night. Then imagine you are in charge of a group of twelve American high schoolers. Finally, imagine that as you begin to fear how your young charges will react to their perilous circumstances, you spy this poster tacked to the wall of the compound you are pacing.

MEMO: REGARDING THE TRANSPORTATION OF DEAD EMPLOYEES

If you are Rob Shafar, youth pastor at Emmanuel Baptist Church in Mt. Vernon, Washington, you wouldn't have to imagine it. You would be *living* it. In Technicolor and Dolby sound.

In 1992 Rob led a missions trip to Kenya to allow his students both to see what "real" missions was like and to help out however they could. One day they intended to make a four-hour drive from Buffalo Springs Tented Camp in the Samburu to Oruz in the Pokot. While that may not strike terror in the hearts of American suburbanites, Kenya is no suburb. Rob likens many of that nation's roads to "your worst driveway gone bad."

Just a few miles out of Buffalo Springs, a tire on the group's minivan blew out. Rob and company had to wait with the van while their missionary hosts returned to get another tire. Several hours later they were on their way again. But after another twenty miles, a second tire blew.

This time the missionaries left Rob and his group at a ranger station while they took off to locate another tire. "Some time after they left us," Rob said, "it occurred to me they drove off with all our money, with all our passports, and with the only people who really knew where we were. *What if they don't come back?* I wondered. *What if they get stuck somewhere—which is eminently feasible in Kenya— and don't return for a day or two? What am I going to do with twelve high school students on a Kenyan ranger station that exists primarily to shoot poachers?*"

Trying to mask his concern, Rob began to wander around the station, looking for something to read. That's when his eye spotted the offending, oversized memo tacked to the wall. Rob shook his head, wondering how big a problem dead employees actually presented. Fortunately, none of his students saw the notice and after a few more hours his group was able to get underway once more. But before they traveled very far, yet another tire disintegrated, and they began the now-familiar drill.

After an unexpected adventure with a man who tried to sell the group his daughter (they weren't in the market),

Rob and his students made camp for the night. Everyone set out their things and lit a campfire. A short while later a vehicle stuffed with about thirty Kenyans stopped and mildly suggested they might not wish to sleep in that particular spot. It seems that herds of elephants used it as a nighttime thoroughfare.

About 1:00 A.M. the missionaries returned. They had taken a little longer than expected because they decided to pick up a second tire, just in case, and had to negotiate its price. Good thing. Between the time they left and the time they returned, yet *another* tire on the minivan gave up the ghost.

If I stay here much longer, Rob must have thought, *I'm going to buy stock in Goodyear.*

When the group finally arrived at Oruz later that day, seven tires in all had gone belly up. Now, most students of that age would have grown testy. But these students had already learned on this trip that God always has a purpose behind everything He does, even when you haven't a clue what it might be. So one of the first things they did upon arriving in Oruz was to seek out Art Davis, the missionary who was to pick them up. "Tell us—why did God delay us? What was He doing here?"

"It's interesting you should ask," Art replied. "I came to the station at the scheduled time to pick you up, but your troubles obviously made it impossible for you to be here. But somebody else was."

Art looked around at the group. "I've spent the past several hours talking to a man who for many years has been openly hostile to the gospel. Before our 'chance meeting' at the station, he simply did not want to hear about Christ. But today…today he *listened*. For hours. Perhaps that explains your seven flat tires; had you arrived on time,

17

I would have missed a golden opportunity to speak to that man about the Lord."

Better than the Funnies

Stories such as Rob's convince me that the Devil proves the old saying, "He can't win for losing." Just when Satan thinks he's masterminded a foolproof plot to devastate the saints, the Lord steps out of the shadows and reveals how *His* battle plan is designed to use the Devil's plot to lift God's children to smashing victory. I'm convinced that if you wrap your mind around this idea, it'll change the way you live. Trying circumstances and devastating blows will no longer have the power to hold you in their awful grip as they once did. Sure, you'll still hurt—that's part of being human, and no book can change that—but you'll be able to look beyond the pain and hurt. You'll know to strain your eyes out toward the horizon, to fix your gaze in expectancy, to search for and hope for and fully anticipate a divine turnabout on *your* behalf. Because that's the sort of God we have.

I was forcefully reminded of this truth years ago when I was editing Herbert Schlossberg's intriguing book, *Called to Suffer, Called to Triumph.* The author wrote about a church in Oriente, Cuba, which for years had asked permission from the Communist government to expand its facilities. After many refusals, the government changed its mind and the church knocked down the walls. At just that point the government changed its mind *again*, reversed it's earlier ruling, and banned all further construction. That left the little church in Oriente with a roof, supporting beams, and no walls. If you were keeping a scorecard, it would certainly have seemed an obvious point for Satan.

Not quite.

18

The author's next words sounded so much like the way God works, I almost laughed out loud when I read them:

But the Lord has used the situation in an interesting way. Since the building has no walls the preaching and hymns are heard in the neighborhood much more clearly than if the church had been enclosed. More people are hearing the gospel this way.[1]

How like God! He takes what appear to be clear victories for the Devil and turns them on their head. He takes Satan's best punch and deflects it back into his own midsection. He transforms detestable situations and events into trophies of His majesty and grace. The night may be black indeed, but there is no night too dark for the Lord to trace a pathway of light through its midst.

In a word, He is the God of turnabouts. He delights in displaying His power and glory and infinite creativity on behalf of His beloved people, for those who have entrusted their souls to the Lord Jesus Christ. If that describes you, you can live with the robust hope that God delights in performing His turnabouts on *your* behalf. For *you*.

I don't expect you to take my word for it, however. In fact, I wouldn't want you to. Scripture is full of incidents which fit this pattern, but allow me to focus on just two, one from each testament.

Losers of the Raided Ark

In the days before Israel had crowned its first king, war raged between the Hebrews and the Philistines. About four thousand Israelites were killed in a fierce battle described in 1 Samuel 4. The disaster prompted the nation's terrified elders to order that the ark of the covenant be brought out from its resting place in Shiloh and carried to the front lines.

They committed the same error Hollywood made in its blockbuster, *Raiders of the Lost Ark.* They assumed the box itself would confer upon them irresistible power. They had forgotten that the ark was merely a shadow, a symbol, of the awesome holiness and might of God Himself. The Israelites foolishly expected the box to give them victory.

When the Philistines heard that the ark had arrived in the Israelite camp, they too fell prey to superstition—but only for awhile. They said,

> A god has come into the camp. We're in trouble! Nothing like this has happened before. Woe to us! Who will deliver us from the hand of these mighty gods? They are the gods who struck the Egyptians with all kinds of plagues in the desert. Be strong, Philistines! Be men, or you will be subject to the Hebrews, as they have been to you. Be men, and fight! (1 Samuel 4:7-9).

They did fight, and they won. In the ensuing battle, thirty thousand Israelite foot soldiers perished. The two sons of the high priest, Eli, were killed—and the ark itself was seized as spoils of war. As chapter 4 draws to a close, the scene is impossibly dark. Eli dies after hearing of the battle and his daughter-in-law quickly follows him after giving premature birth to a son. The chapter ends with these dismal words:

> Then she murmured, "Name the child 'Ichabod,' for Israel's glory is gone." (Ichabod means "there is no glory." She named him this because the Ark of God had been captured and because her husband and her father-in-law were dead) (1 Samuel 4:21-22, TLB).

In all of Israel's long, checkered history, it's hard to find a more somber scene.

Meanwhile, the Philistines exulted. Danced. Partied. Slapped high fives. Not only had they crushed Israel in battle, but events had proven their gods stronger than the God of the Jews. Or so they thought. Such would be a logical deduction in the world of the ancient Near East. It seemed that Yahweh, the God of Israel, was no more than a two-bit deity for losers.

The Philistines took the ark and set it up as a trophy in the temple of their own god, Dagon. They went to sleep with dreams of sweet conquest. Then the morning dawned, and with it a shock—Dagon had fallen on his face before the ark! Supposing this to be an unfortunate accident (but possibly a bit ill at ease), the Philistines set Dagon back in his place. But the next morning, they found Dagon licking dust once again—this time, with his head and hands broken off and lying on the threshold. A chill swept the populace.

They didn't know it, but God had just begun a classic turnabout.

This odd nighttime event soon exploded into a daytime nightmare. A plague broke out among the inhabitants of Ashdod, where the ark had been taken, and the people instantly recognized its cause: "The ark of the god of Israel must not stay here with us, because his hand is heavy upon us and upon Dagon our god," they said (1 Samuel 5:7).

So they did what any good pagan would do: they sent the ark to their neighbors. The plague followed. After brief appearances in Ashdod, Gath, and Ekron, the Philistines had suffered enough.

21

> So they summoned the mayors again and begged them to send the Ark back to its own country, lest the entire city die. For the plague had already begun and great fear was sweeping across the city. Those who didn't die were deathly ill; and there was weeping everywhere (1 Samuel 5:11-12, TLB).

After seven months of misery, the Philistines returned the ark to Israel, laden with golden offerings. They did this to "pay honor to Israel's god" and in hopes that He would lift His hand from them and their gods and their land (1 Samuel 6:5). At last they had learned their puny gods were no match for the Lord of all the earth—not even when a military triumph appeared to suggest the opposite.

Let's not miss what this story teaches. There is no question that Israel's defeat in battle was a dreadful thing. It is certain that the capture of the ark marked a low point in the nation's history. Without doubt the surrounding peoples reasoned that Israel's defeat and the seizure of God's ark meant Dagon was mightier than Yahweh.

But God took that very evil and turned it on its head. It was precisely the ark's seven-month captivity in Philistia that proved God's supremacy.

A Jail That Couldn't Imprison

22

The apostle Paul knew all about God's taste for reversing the diabolical spin Satan schemes to put on crucial events. Paul knew that when evil mushrooms, it's time to look for some divine fungicide.

A wonderful illustration of this can be found in the little book of Philippians. This book rings with praise and joy, so much so that it inspired best-selling author Chuck Swindoll to write a book titled *Laugh Again*.

But the circumstances leading up to the writing of Philippians are anything but funny. Paul had been arrested for preaching the gospel. Once he had been free to roam about the Roman world, propagating the Good News of Jesus Christ; now he was chained to a Roman soldier, prevented from spreading the Word of God.

Or was he?

It's true, he was chained to a Roman guard. In fact, it's probable these guards relieved each other at regular duty intervals. So Paul was not free to range far and wide to proclaim the gospel as he had formerly. But what do you suppose Paul would talk about with Rome's finest? After hours of being chained to the dedicated evangelist, no doubt some soldiers would begin wondering just who was captive to vhom. And in fact, that is apparently just what happened:

> Now I want you to know, brothers, that what has happened to me has really served to advance the gospel. As a result, it has become clear throughout the whole palace guard and to everyone else that I am in chains for Christ (Philippians 1:12-13).

Once again, God had taken a clear victory for the Devil—Satan's imprisonment of an effective evangelist— and turned that very evil into a triumph of His grace. What better way to evangelize tough Roman soldiers, than to get down and dirty with them in close quarters over extended periods of time?

23

I think that would be enough to qualify as an awesome turnabout, but God wasn't done. Paul then said:

> Because of my chains, most of the brothers in the Lord have been encouraged to speak the word of God more courageously and fearlessly (1:14).

Notice: it is *because* of Paul's chains that the Word of God went out boldly! I doubt that's what Satan had in mind when Paul was tossed into prison.

My, what a headache Satan created for himself! Not only did his attack make a way for the hard hearts of grizzled Roman soldiers to be softened by the gospel of grace, but it enabled God to create scores of evangelists where once there had been just poor, lonely Paul!

Anyone planning to oppose the King of the Universe should take note: When you're dealing with the God of turnabouts, you can't be too careful.

What About You?

So far we've talked a lot about what God has done in the lives of others to turn evil situations into surprises of His grace. I hope this has encouraged you; but I also suspect that some of you may be tempted to think it could never happen in *your* case. Your situation is too desperate. Too dark. Too grim. It has continued for too long and has sunk too deep for you to cherish any hope of rescue. Yes, God may be a God of turnabouts—but not in your case.

If that's your conviction, let me encourage you to think again. While I can't guarantee that God will turn around your situation in the same way He did for Paul or in the case of the ark, I do know that, if you are His child, you are at the center of His thoughts. Your name is inscribed on the very palms of His hands (Isaiah 49:15-16) and He loves you with an everlasting love. One day all your pain and tears will be wiped away and you will bask forever in the limitless goodness and grace of almighty God. You will share an eternal inheritance with Jesus and will taste of divine pleasures forevermore.

"Aha," you may say, "I knew it. You're telling me I have no hope except for the world to come, so I might as well get used to the dungeon in this one." No, that's not what I'm saying. I said I couldn't *guarantee* that God will perform a turnabout for you; but I think the likelihood is, He will.

I've saved a discussion of why God delights in turnabouts for later, but for now let me say this: The darker the situation, the more likely it is that God will pull His rabbit out of the hat (or better, that he will turn a wolf into a rabbit!).

Turnabouts show more clearly than anything else the supremacy and majesty of God. The more difficult the situation, the more plain God's turnabouts make it that He alone rules the universe.

So take heart! While God chooses when and where He performs His turnabouts, desperate situations are made-to-order for divine turnabouts. And when they happen, you'll be left breathless. Just as others already have discovered.

In God's Bermuda Triangle

Much has been written about the mysteries of the Bermuda Triangle, a vaguely triangular patch of ocean stretching from the southern U.S. coast to Bermuda to the Greater Antilles. According to legend, ships disappear without a trace, airplanes vanish, UFOs use the area as a home base, and similar otherworldly phenomena occur there with chilling regularity.

Regardless of the truth of these reports, however, it is certain that one corner of the triangle has in the past few months witnessed some extraordinary, hard-to-believe events. God appears to be in the midst of pulling off a classic turnabout.

Cuba—that bastion of communism in the Western Hemisphere, that nation which made it hard for the church in Oriente—is opening up to the gospel.

Elmer Thompson, co-founder of Worldteam, was in Cuba recently and was astonished at what he saw:

> Everyone in Cuba is awake—not converted, but awake—and searching for God. I saw unsaved people run up to Christians and ask to be led to Christ. I saw this happen! This kind of thing has taken place before in the world. It has happened in American history, too. But it has never appeared around me.[2]

25

George Otis, Jr. and the staff of the Sentinel Group also have been amazed by recent events in Cuba. Otis filed this report in a special edition of *Charisma* magazine:

> Just six years ago, churches in Cuba were languishing under Fidel Castro's regime of fear and intimidation. Only a few older people were willing to be identified as Christians, and they felt isolated and forgotten by the rest of the world. Bibles were scarce, religious broadcasting was not permitted, and Castro was still attempting to turn his impoverished island nation into an atheistic paradise.
>
> Today, although Castro remains in power, the tables have turned. A religious resurgence is sweeping the country, Bible sales are booming, and thousands of new believers are filling up Pentecostal, Baptist and Catholic churches. After loosening the ban on religion last year, Castro recently admitted he made a mistake when he tried to force atheism on his people.[3]

No wonder the dictator thinks he made a mistake! Spontaneous meetings of Christians are now occurring at all hours of the day and night throughout his country. One three-week evangelistic campaign resulted in twenty-two thousand professions of faith in Christ and the Assemblies of God alone have begun about four hundred house churches in the past few years. More Bibles have been distributed in the past two years than in the previous thirty, and some observers claim informal house churches now outnumber traditional congregations by three to one. Young people are flocking to churches and people are more open to the gospel than perhaps ever before. "Churches that used to be half-full are having services three or four times a day," said one source. "Young people who have been indoctrinated by communism are seeing the power of God in the church."[4]

Cuba alone proves that God can work His turnabouts wherever and whenever He chooses. Try to close down a church in Oriente by wrecking its facilities? Fine. More people will come to the Lord that way. Try to force atheism on a people who don't want it? Fine. In the end, they will stampede to hear the gospel.

You don't have to travel to Cuba, however, to see how God uses the Devil's very worst schemes to promote the kingdom of God. Examples abound.

Vera Mae Perkins, the wife of evangelist and social activist John Perkins, has lived divine turnabouts. After describing how her husband was beaten in Mississippi jails, how her family was refused service at motels because of race, and how difficult it could be to rear eight kids on little money, she writes:

> Our struggles were painful, but I grew to expect them and—believe it or not—even appreciate them. Many young couples, especially wives, believe that suffering should be avoided at all costs—that God wouldn't want them or their children to suffer. Although this is a natural inclination, it is very far from the truth. Suffering builds character and faith. Many times God calls us to a life that includes suffering. John and I find that suffering together through hard times makes us depend on each other more, and binds us closer together.[5]

27

You'd think the Devil would learn: take a whack, get it back. But the message never seems to register.

Joanne Shetler, a missionary with Wycliffe Bible Translators to the Balangao people of the Philippines, has seen this principle in action many times. But often, the

Devil wasn't the only one who failed to "get it." She did, too. God's turnabouts are so surprising, so unusual, so divine that we don't see them coming. Happily, however, we can rejoice once the muck has cleared from our eyes!

For many months, Shetler had longed for the Balangao Christians to grow past their short, perfunctory prayers:

> I'd often awaken in the middle of the night, begging God to teach them to pray. I'd written home asking friends to pray: "The believers need to learn to pray with intensity. They need to understand that their own powers are useless, even in doing 'godly' things, and that only what God performs will be real in people's lives...." If there is a longing in my heart, it is that God would make these Balangaos a people of effective, powerful prayer.[6]

Joanne then uttered a desperate prayer herself. "God," she said, "I don't care what you have to do; make these people pray!"

28

Some time later she received the answer to her prayer. Shetler and Dr. Robespierre Lim were about to touch down in a helicopter full of supplies earmarked for building the Balangao's first hospital when they hit a tree and crashed. Shetler began to panic when she realized the extent of her injuries. But what caused her real terror was the thought that she might die before she could finish translating the Bible into the language of the Balangaos.

As fuel spilled from a big gash in the craft and flames leapt from the remains of the rotor blades, she heard voices yelling to get back, that the helicopter was about to explode. But when the Balangaos realized Shetler was alive and still inside, they rushed back to the accident, doused the craft with mud and water, and put out the flames.

Shetler's rescuers were appalled when they pulled her

from the wreckage and got their first glimpse of her. Her ribs were broken and one lung had collapsed. Her eyes had filled with powdered cement during her unconsciousness and the caustic lime in the cement ate into the soft tissue. Her eyes felt as if they were on fire.

Some Balangaos thought her condition hopeless: "Can't you see she's already dead—just her breath is left."[7]

It was far from hopeless, however. In fact, God was about to spring a mountain-sized turnabout on the Balangao people. It took Shetler completely by surprise.

> The night was long, the pain intense. But something else was going on. Something new for Balangaos. One by one, throughout the night, Balangao Christians worked their way through the throng, touched my hand, and prayed. I'll never forget their prayers: "God, don't let her die, the Book's not done yet. Just let her live; the Book's not done yet."

> That night, as I lay on the floor, more dead than alive, the Balangaos were praying—really praying. One after another, they prayed the same prayer, "Don't let her die, the Book's not done yet."

> It was the worst and best night of my life all wrapped up in one. The worst pain I'd ever known was eclipsed by moments of indescribable awe over their prayers. Only God could weave such extremes.[8]

29

That's the secret! "Only God can weave such extremes." Only God can take the extremes of your life—the desperate and the delightful—and craft them into a turnabout too exquisite for words. Only God can do that! In a snap. In the twinkle of His eye. Our loving heavenly Father delights in deflecting Satan's best shots back into his own face. Friends, when God puts up His dukes, it's a KO in .03 seconds.

Why? Because He is the God of turnabouts. In Cuba, in Kenya, in Mississippi, in the Philippines... wherever His kids live. And that includes your address, too.

> Now to him who is able to do immeasurably more than all we ask or imagine, according to his power that is at work within us, to him be glory in the church and in Christ Jesus throughout all generations, for ever and ever! Amen (Ephesians 3:20-21).

Chapter 2

Righteous Reversals

Okay, I admit it. I'm an avid fan of TV's *Star Trek: The Next Generation*. I've also started to watch a spin-off, *Star Trek: Deep Space Nine*. I've been fascinated by science fiction since junior high school and believe these shows (with several notable exceptions) generally do a good job of translating exotic ideas from books to the small screen.

You're apt to meet all kinds of creatures from many distant stars in these episodes, but few are as intriguing as the beings called "shape shifters." Shape shifters—or "elasso-morphs," for the technically-minded—can change shape, size, color, and even mass at will. You want to look like a human? Poof! No problem. A rat? Poof! It's done. In one early episode of *Deep Space Nine*, Odo, a shape-shifting security officer, changed himself into a leather chair and waited unnoticed in a suspect's living quarters until the culprit arrived. His spectacular metamorphosis bore little resemblance to the cheesy special effects of the original *Star Trek*.

I mention shape-shifters for one reason only. No, I'm not going to say that God is like a shape-shifter. Hardly! An infinite gulf is forever fixed between Him and all creatures, however remarkable they might be. God is no shape-shifter—*but His turnabouts are.*

Just when you think you have this business of turnabouts figured out, another one hurtles through your back door in a form and guise unlooked for. Just when you believe you know how God must act in a certain situation, POOF! The turnabout shifts shape before your unbelieving eyes.

But the same God is always behind them all.

In the last chapter we saw how God delights in using what seem to be clear victories for the Devil and stands them on their heads, changing them into triumphs for God's people. He uses the very evil itself to display His dazzling glory.

Not all of His turnabouts are like that, however. Just when you've come to recognize that delightful pattern, POOF! The turnabout shifts shape into another equally wonderful form.

I was reminded of this recently while reading about the infant church in parts of the Middle East. The church in Saudi Arabia received an unexpected boost in the wake of Operation Desert Storm, the U.N.'s response to Iraqi strongman Saddam Hussein's invasion of Kuwait. Bibles and testaments flooded into the country, and many people for the first time were confronted with the true message of Christianity.

Naturally, this news was not greeted with joy by hardline Muslims. In fact, the Metawwa, an eight thousand-member religious police force claiming to answer to Allah alone, decided it was time to clamp down hard on Christian activity. The group scheduled a secret meeting in Riyadh which focused on how to identify and disrupt Christian activities in the country, how to stake out and report on Christian gatherings, and how to collect rewards. But it made a crucial mistake; it forgot that the Christian God is a God of turnabouts.

Among those invited to the meeting was a Sudanese whom the Metawwa assumed was a Muslim. He wasn't. He was a dedicated Christian whom God immediately enlisted in the F.B.I. (the Father's Bureau of Infiltration). The magazine report detailing this incident concluded "as a consequence of this divinely arranged infiltration, Christian fellowships in recent months have been able to take protective countermeasures."[1]

In other words, a clandestine meeting designed to cause trouble for Christians instead was transformed into a vehicle for their protection.

Welcome to the topsy-turvy world of Righteous Reversals.

From Head Advisor to Dead Downsizer

Perhaps the clearest biblical example of this species of divine turnabout is the remarkable account found in the book of Esther. For in this incident, instead of using the evil for His glory, God reversed it altogether. Satan never put a glove on God's people; in effect, Lucifer bloodied his lip with a clear shot to his own jaw.

But it didn't start out that way.

The events described in Esther took place following Israel's seventy years of captivity in Babylon. Although some Jews returned to their homeland after Cyrus conquered Babylon in 539 B.C., many remained scattered throughout the vast Persian empire. One of those Jews was

Esther, the beautiful young cousin of Mordecai. Esther was an orphan, and Mordecai reared her as if he were her own father. The story is rich in irony and in illustrations of God's providence, and only a thorough reading of the book itself does it justice. But allow me to briefly recap the story's highlights.

Esther's stunning beauty inevitably attracted the attention of the royal palace and she soon became queen. At almost the same time, Mordecai overheard a plot to assassinate the king and reported it to Esther, who informed Xerxes. Mordecai's allegiance was faithfully recorded in the official palace archives.

Some time later Haman, who enjoyed "a seat of honor higher than that of all the other nobles" (Esther 3:1), became furious with Mordecai for a perceived snub. Immediately he began to plot vengeance:

> When Haman saw that Mordecai would not kneel
> down or pay him honor, he was enraged. Yet having
> learned who Mordecai's people were, he scorned the
> idea of killing only Mordecai. Instead Haman looked
> for a way to destroy all Mordecai's people, the Jews,
> throughout the whole kingdom of Xerxes (3:5-6).

Soon Haman convinced the king that it would be in his best interest to eradicate the Jews. Dispatches were sent to all corners of the kingdom "with the order to destroy, kill and annihilate all the Jews—young and old, women and little children—on a single day, the thirteenth day of the twelfth month, the month of Adar, and to plunder their goods" (3:13).

When Mordecai heard the news, he tore his clothes, donned sackcloth and ashes, and wailed bitterly. Esther, who had not received word of the King's edict, became alarmed when she learned of her uncle's behavior. After she had been fully informed, she and her uncle developed a plan of action based on a piece of vital information unknown to Haman:

Esther, too, was a Jew.

Part of the plan called for Esther to invite Xerxes and Haman to a series of lavish banquets. The king was delighted with this royal treatment and grew anxious to grant Esther her fondest wish; but Esther refrained until just the right moment. Haman was equally thrilled with the invitation and boasted to his friends:

> "I'm the only person Queen Esther invited to accompany the king to the banquet she gave. And she has invited me along with the king tomorrow. But all this gives me no satisfaction as long as I see that Jew Mordecai sitting at the king's gate."

> His wife Zeresh and all his friends said to him, "Have a gallows built, seventy-five feet high, and ask the king in the morning to have Mordecai hanged on it. Then go with the king to the dinner and be happy." This suggestion delighted Haman, and he had the gallows built (5:12-14).

That night the king could not sleep and so ordered that the record of his administration be read to him. The book recounted Mordecai's exposé of the assassination plot against the king, and Xerxes was chagrined to learn that nothing had been done to honor the man. Just then Haman entered the outer court of the palace intending to ask that Mordecai be hanged. The king invited Haman into the throne room and asked what ought to be done for someone the king wanted to highly honor. Haman thought the king spoke of Haman, and so answered,

For the man the king delights to honor, have them bring a royal robe the king has worn and a horse the king has ridden, one with a royal crest placed on its head. Then let the robe and horse be entrusted to one of the king's most noble princes. Let them robe the man the king delights to honor, and lead him on the horse through the city streets, proclaiming before him, "This is what is done for the man the king delights to honor!" (6:7-9).

The king judged the idea splendid and ordered Haman to carry out his plan immediately—in honor of Mordecai the Jew.

A humiliated Haman did as he was told, then rushed home and spilled the awful news to his wife and friends. It is doubtful they held certifications in counseling: "Since Mordecai, before whom your downfall has started, is of Jewish origin, you cannot stand against him—you will surely come to ruin!" (6:13).

Counselors, no. Prophets, yes. And so the bell brought Round One to an end in this Old Testament Righteous Reversal. Round Two—a decisive one—would immediately follow.

Haman had no sooner poured out his grief to his friends and family than he was whisked away to Esther's banquet. King Xerxes again pled to know what his queen might request of him. This time, she answered:

If I have found favor with you, O king, and if it pleases your majesty, grant me my life—this is my petition. And spare my people—this is my request. For I and my people have been sold for destruction and slaughter and annihilation. If we had merely been sold as male and female slaves, I would have kept quiet, because no such distress would justify disturbing the king (7:3-4).

The king exploded in anger and demanded to know who would dare to threaten his lovely queen. "The adversary and enemy is this vile Haman," Esther replied (7:6).

Xerxes got up in a rage and stalked off to his garden to allow his anger to cool. Haman felt the hangman's noose tightening around his neck and stayed behind to beg Esther for his life. Just as he threw himself on her royal couch, Xerxes returned. "Will he even molest the queen while she is with me in the house?" he stormed. The final words of chapter seven mark the official end of Round Two:

> As soon as the word left the king's mouth, they covered Haman's face. Then Harbona, one of the eunuchs attending the king, said, "A gallows seventy-five feet high stands by Haman's house. He had it made for Mordecai, who spoke up to help the king."

> The king said, "Hang him on it!" So they hanged Haman on the gallows he had prepared for Mordecai. Then the king's fury subsided (7:8b-10).

37

Only one problem remained. The king's edict to destroy the Jews could not be rescinded, since "no document written in the king's name and sealed with his ring can be revoked" (8:8). But another decree could be issued, one giving the Jews the right to defend themselves. That order was given and suddenly a new day had dawned:

> For the Jews it was a time of happiness and joy, gladness and honor. In every province and in every city, wherever the edict of the king went, there was joy and gladness among the Jews, with feasting and celebrating. And many people of other nationalities became Jews because fear of the Jews had seized them (8:16-17).

Time to check your scorecards, boxing fans. Round Three is over, the knockout punch has been delivered. And *the* classic Righteous Reversal was in the books.

The *New Bible Commentary* sums it up as well as anyone. J. G. Baldwin wrote:

> In an unforseeable way, circumstances so fell out that Haman became the victim of his own plot, the Jews were delivered, their enemies were liquidated, and a Jew [Mordecai] was appointed to the position of greatest influence next to the king. This miraculous reversal of affairs was celebrated throughout the Persian Empire, and is still celebrated annually by Jews in every part of the world at the festival known as Purim.[2]

I have a suggestion for all Jewish households across the world who annually celebrate the feast of Purim—and please know that I mean no disrespect. Just as the meal is about to be served, the guests should solemnly rise, pick up the table, and turn it all the way around, end for end. That, after all, is what God did for them.

Present-Day Reversals

Sometimes, God's turnabouts are like that. He permits the night to grow inky black before He swallows the darkness in the sudden brilliance of a supernova. He allows wickedness to smack its lips over a dish of roasted saints just before the Heavenly Health Department moves in, closes down the vile establishment, and sets out a banquet table for the faithful to feast upon.

God is an expert at Righteous Reversals. He knows just when they're needed and brings them out of the storehouse of His turnabouts at precisely the right time.

38

It may be that you need such a reversal right now. The darkness is closing in and you boast no power to dispel the gloom. Friend, while I can't guarantee that God will perform a Righteous Reversal on your behalf, I do know that He will do exactly the right thing at precisely the best hour. Your life is not left to chance; you are not dangling in the wind. You can fully expect that God *will* deliver you. But the manner of His deliverance and His timing can never be clearly predicted.

But do me this favor, would you? Should He stretch out His mighty hand and turn upside down and inside out some Satanic scheme that threatens your world, should He prove to you that no night is too dark for His light to break through, then take a few moments alone to praise the Lord of Glory…and then open your mouth in public adoration so others may stand amazed at the God of turnabouts. It's exactly because others did open their mouths that I can recount for you some of their stories.

Wrestling Is His Sport, Too

God won the boxing match in the story of Esther and Mordecai, but He is not limited to that sport; His wrestling talents are equally prodigious.

This was made plain at a recent seminar of the Institute in Basic Life Principles held in Seattle. Five thousand attendees were shocked when a young man ran up on stage and attempted to disrupt the meeting. "What followed," said an IBLP newsletter, "demonstrated the mighty power of God." It also illustrated His fondness for Righteous Reversals.

Leaders immediately ushered the young man back stage and entered into a twenty-minute battle of "spiritual warfare" with him. At the end of that time, the man was freed from "strongholds" of bitterness and immorality.

Then this young man and his father were asked if they would like to give the audience a testimony of praise to God. They said yes.

The meeting was paused and "to the delight and amazement of the entire audience," this father and son walked out onto the stage where just moments before the Evil One had tried to wreck the seminar and "told of how God had freed the young man from the bondage of Satan."[3]

God froze the evil in its tracks and reversed it, to the glory of His matchless name. The Lord pinned Satan to the mat almost before he stepped into the circle.

From Seattle to Vietnam

All over the world and in the lives of countless of His precious children, God is showing His might by reversing Satan's evil schemes before they can take root to choke out the lives of faithful believers.

A recent story from Vietnam illustrates God's fondness for Righteous Reversals. Communist leaders had learned of an outbreak of religious fervency in an area where an evangelist had been preaching. Party officials became alarmed and so dispatched several "teachers" to conduct a six-hour "re-education campaign" in a village situated in the highlands:[4]

> At the end of the session, one of the officials strode to the blackboard and scribbled two headings: "Against Christ" and "For Christ." He then asked the villagers to write their names in the appropriate column. The people sat motionless as they pondered how to respond.
>
> Finally, an elderly woman who had previously served as a Marxist spokesperson in the village addressed

the group. "For the past 20 years I have followed Marxism," she said. "I have followed the party line and served as your leader. But a few months ago, I came to realize that Jesus Christ offers a better way." She then signed her name as one who was "For Christ." As the chagrined cadres watched, the entire village took her cue and followed suit.[5]

How can you read such an account and not break into a smile? God took a potentially devastating predicament and transformed it into an overpowering witness for the truth of the gospel. And whom did He choose to put at center stage? A woman who formerly led the opposition to His kingdom! Shades of Haman and Mordecai! Truly, He is a God of turnabouts.

But it gets even better. If you're not smiling now, I think the corners of your mouth will elevate in a few moments. This is how the report concludes:

A denominational field representative familiar with this account reports that government officials are baffled by the move of God in the area. He relates that an early 1992 article translated from a Vietnamese newspaper concluded: "We don't know what is happening [in the Highlands], but it is something called the 'Good News' religion."[6]

41

Good News? You bet! Good News that Jesus Christ took on human flesh, died for our sins, and rose from the dead, never to die again. Good News that we can enter into His life through faith in His name. Good News that He still sits at the helm of the universe, directing its course until the pre-ordained consummation of all things. And yes, Good News that sometimes His actions baffle human understanding. And that includes the understanding of Christians.

We, too, can be baffled by what God does. But we should never be completely surprised. For although His character never changes, His methods oftentimes do. The varieties of His turnabouts seem endless. The shape-shifting critters just won't keep one form long enough for us to get a bead on them.

Fortunately, we don't have to. *They* have the bead on us.

Chapter 3

Special Delivery

---

*U*ntil the last century or so, anyone who wanted a message or package delivered quickly to an address hundreds of miles away was just out of luck. It couldn't be done. Delivery times were measured in weeks and months, not days or hours.

That began to change in the United States in April 1860 when the Pony Express, a system of mail delivery by continuous horse and rider relays, began operation between St. Joseph, Missouri, and Sacramento, California. The approximately eighteen hundred-mile route, which ordinarily would take weeks to travel, could now be covered in about ten days. Riders such as William "Buffalo Bill" Cody changed horses six to eight times between 157 stations. The completion of a transcontinental telegraph system in October 1861 doomed the immensely unprofitable Pony Express, but a precedent had been set.

Within a few years the United States Postal Service developed a system for handling urgent mail. For an extra fee, the Postal Service would deliver such mail by a special messenger as soon as it arrived at the receiving post office. From 1885 until 1979, there was only one place to find such service and only one name under which it could be secured: Special Delivery by the U.S. Postal Service. Since 1979 several companies have entered the urgent mail business, but the term "special delivery" has stuck.

Other countries have similar systems. Canada offers a service called "assured mail delivery" which guarantees overnight mail service to any part of the country. Great Britain uses traveling post offices aboard trains that criss-cross the nation at night. And several major European cities such as Paris, Marseilles, and Rome whisk important materials to their destinations within two hours through the use of a pneumatic tube system called a *pneumatique*.

44

What all of these systems recognize is the necessity of rapid service for urgent needs. Some messages and some projects are so momentous that they can't wait for ordinary delivery schedules; they require instant attention and extraordinary handling. Without special delivery, the message spoils and the project disintegrates.

Unfortunately, all special delivery systems eventually break down.

Just a few weeks ago, I was working on a project that "absolutely, positively, *had* to be there" at a remote site by early afternoon. I missed the usual quick-delivery companies and was forced to go with Plan B. I chose a regional airline that promised delivery within a couple of hours, paid their higher-than-normal fee, and returned home with the assurance that I had met my deadline. But several hours later I received a phone call from those who needed the package. It hadn't arrived. A quick call to the airline revealed that not only was the package undelivered, the company didn't know where it was. Immediately an old joke rushed into my mind: A man heading for Los Angeles stands at the airline counter with his luggage. "Three bags to check, sir?" asks the counter attendant.

"Yes," replies the man, "and I'd like this one to go to Tokyo, that one to Rome, and the third sent to Buenos Aires."

"Sir, I'm sorry, but we can't do that," the employee responds apologetically.

"Why not?" the man demands, "that's what you did the last time I flew with you."

I don't know what exotic locations my package might have visited, but I do know it didn't arrive any more quickly than had I sent it by conventional transport. And while the delay didn't cripple the project, it did seriously upset a tight schedule.

45

Human special delivery systems are like that: prone to break down, misfire, and threaten the projects dearest to our hearts. Much of the time, these system can be relied upon. But every once in awhile, when you can't afford the slightest delay, a package intended for Des Moines winds up in Petropavlovsk-Kamchatsky.

The good news is that God operates a special delivery system, too, and it eternally functions at 100 percent efficiency. His packages never get lost, never fall behind schedule, never become damaged in transport or spoil en route. Packages addressed to Des Moines are received by Hawkeyes, not Russians.

Even so, don't be fooled into thinking God's special delivery service operates without surprises. His packages arrive on time—His time—but we never know when to expect them. I should probably mention that it's not so much *what* He delivers as *who*. For God's special delivery service is chartered to "deliver" His children from certain disaster; that's what makes it "special."

You see, in God's urgent mail company, you're not only the package recipient, you're the package. It's *you* He delivers.

He's Not on Welfare

It's all too easy in a man-centered culture like ours to forget just how infinite is the distance between God and ourselves. We are so impressed with our burgeoning technological and scientific advancements that we lose sight of the awesome majesty and holiness and power and glory of God. We begin to feel there's really not so much difference between the Creator and the created. That's why a text such as Psalm 50 can so startle us.

Psalm 50 confronts us with a God so supreme, so invincible, so utterly unlike ourselves that with a mere word He summons both the earth and the heavens. It brings us face-to-face with an almighty Judge before Whom a fire devours and a tempest rages. It pictures a God so self-sufficient that, were it possible, He sounds almost arrogant. Listen to this God speak:

I have no need of a bull from your stall
    or of goats from your pens,
for every animal of the forest is mine,
    and the cattle on a thousand hills.
I know every bird in the mountains,
    and the creatures of the feild are mine.
If I were hungry I would not tell you,
    for the world is mine, and all that is in it
        (Psalm 50:9-12).

In all our investigation of divine turnabouts, this is the God in view. "The LORD does whatever pleases him, in the heavens and on the earth, in the seas and all their depths" (Psalm 135:6). That being so, it seems almost incomprehensible that such a self-sufficient, omnipotent, untamable God should take great pleasure in coming to the rescue of poor, weak, woe-begone human beings who so often seem to stumble headlong into bottomless pits.

We all like to fancy ourselves as powerful, decisive, take-charge types who overcome all obstacles threatening our progress. And sometimes we manage to convince others that such a picture is accurate. But inevitably circumstances overwhelm us and the flimsy, dried mud walls of our hand-made fortresses come tumbling down in the teeth of a raging thunderstorm. It is then that we cry out for a stronger hand to rescue us.

And amazingly, it does.

Psalm 50 not only pictures an unstoppable, juggernaut deity of infinite power and authority, but a Heavenly Father who delights in delivering His children from hair-raising calamities. After the Lord has made plain His standing as King of the Universe, He adds this line: "call upon me in the day of trouble; I will deliver you, and you will honor me" (50:15).

47

You might call Psalm 50:15 the 1-800 number of Heaven's Special Delivery Service. The call is free ("call upon Me"), it's for urgent packages ("in the day of trouble"), and is guaranteed ("I will deliver you"). A payment plan is even detailed: "and you will honor Me."

Call that number, and expect to see a heavenly delivery van pull up to your curb, the company's slogan etched in gold letters on the van's side: CALL UPON ME—I DELIVER.

Charles Haddon Spurgeon once preached on this text:

God and the praying man take shares.... First, here
is your share: "Call upon me in the day of trouble."
Secondly, here is God's share: "I will deliver thee."
Again, you take a share—for you shall be delivered.
And then again it is the Lord's turn—"Thou shalt
glorify me." Here is a compact, a covenant that God
enters into with you who pray to him, and whom he
helps. He says, "You shall have the deliverance, but
I must have the glory...." Here is a delightful partnership: we obtain that which we so greatly need,
and all that God getteth is the glory which is due
unto his name.[1]

The kind of turnabout detailed in Psalm 50:15 warms
our heart and fuels our hope. For there are times when the
skies grow so dark and the enemy so menacing that, should
God withhold His hand, we would surely perish...and there
would be no turnabout for which to give God glory. The
famous Reformer Martin Luther certainly knew an ominous
day like that.

48

Recant Or Die

Martin Luther was the German monk who on October
31, 1517, unintentionally touched off a firestorm that eventually incinerated Rome's monolithic control of the Christian
church. His posting of Ninety-five Theses on the church
door at Wittenberg is well known, as is his heroic speech
before hostile delegates to the Diet of Worms in 1521.

But what is perhaps not so well known is the story of
what happened to Luther immediately following his triumph
at Worms. It is a classic account of divine turnabout (Special
Delivery subdivision). But to fully understand the reformer's
dire circumstances, we have to back up a bit.

Luther in 1517 had just begun to challenge the practices and authority of the pope. He did not intend to start a new church, but to reform the one he was in. In the years between his theses and the Diet of Worms, however, enormous differences of belief and intemperate statements on both sides made that impossible. By the time Luther was summoned to appear before state and religious leaders at Worms to recant his beliefs and writings, he had been excommunicated several times.

Aleander, one of the two Italian legates at Worms representing the pope, called Luther a "fool," a "dog," a "basilisk," and a "ribald," strongly urged the burning of his books, and threatened, "If ye Germans who pay least into the Pope's treasury shake off his yoke, we shall take care that ye mutually kill yourselves, and wade in your own blood."[2]

Sounds like some church business meetings I've heard about. This was not a pleasant walk in the park.

The Emperor Charles, who had summoned Luther to Worms, was torn between political and religious interests and did not know what to do with the reformer. If he handed him over to Rome, he risked armed rebellion in Germany. If he failed to repudiate Luther, he risked a dangerous falling out with the pope.

49

On April 2, 1521, Luther and three friends set out for Worms from Wittenberg, riding in an open farmer's wagon. He honestly hoped he would be allowed to defend his positions before a final judgment was made; but just before he left his home town, the emperor ordered the reformer's books seized and forbade their sale. Luther would not find the Diet an unbiased tribunal.

Luther arrived in Worms on April 16 and was summoned before the Diet the next day. As he surveyed the impressive gathering of state and religious leaders, his confidence momentarily sagged. When asked if he would retract his books, Luther answered in a voice so low it was almost inaudible. He asked for further time for consideration, "since it involved the salvation of the soul, and the truth of the word of God, which was higher than anything else in heaven or in earth."[3]

The emperor granted him another day, and a gleeful Aleander reported to Rome that Luther entered laughing and left despondent.

On April 18 Luther was again summoned before the Diet. This time, when asked whether he would recant his books, Luther answered with the famous words, "Unless I am refuted and convicted by testimonies of the Scriptures or by clear arguments (since I believe neither the Pope nor the councils alone; it being evident that they have often erred and contradicted themselves), I am conquered by the Holy Scriptures quoted by me, and my conscience is bound in the word of God: I can not and will not recant any thing, since it is unsafe and dangerous to do any thing against the conscience." It is unclear whether Luther actually spoke the following words, but they would be a fitting conclusion: "Here I stand. I can not do otherwise. God help me! Amen."[4]

Luther's questioning of the church councils irked Charles and the emperor finally decided to treat Luther as an obstinate and convicted heretic. Private negotiations between Luther and Charles failed to reconcile their positions, and on April 25 Luther asked permission to return home.

The trip would be the most perilous of the reformer's life.

Luther and all his friends recognized the danger. For although the emperor had promised Luther safe conduct home, such assurances hadn't protected others whom Rome wanted dead. Just one hundred years before, a Czech reformer by the name of John Hus had been summoned to a similar Diet and was promised safe conduct by the emperor —but he had been seized, condemned, and burned at the stake as a heretic. And in fact, Rome had made provision to seize Luther just as it had Hus.[5]

Shortly after the tribunal, Charles signed a papal bull which condemned Luther as a devil in the dress of a monk. Philip Schaff, author of a majestic history of the Christian church, summarized Luther's predicament.

> Thus Luther was outlawed by Church and State, condemned by the Pope, the Emperor, the universities, cast out of human society, and left exposed to a violent death.[6]

So it was on April 26 that Luther began a slow trek back home. He stayed with friends and relatives on the way and preached often, although the emperor had forbidden him to do so. He knew his life hung by a thread but he refused to flee as friends had advised.

And then the fateful day arrived.

On May 4 Luther and his group were surprised by a band of armed horsemen who suddenly rushed from the woods. In a chaos of cursing and swearing and terrible confusion, the men intercepted Luther's carriage, yanked him out, forced him on horseback, and fled with him at full speed.

It happened in broad daylight, but to Luther's companions it seemed as if darkness had dropped like a curtain. Luther's worried friends apparently had been right; his appointment with the stake could now be only hours away—and there was nothing they could do about it.

Luther and his abductors rode in silence until about midnight, when the reformer learned he had been taken to the castle at Wartburg where he would be detained as a prisoner of state in charge of Captain von Berlepsch.

It was turnabout time. God's angels had just made a remarkable special delivery.

Luther hadn't been seized by enemies from Rome after all. He had been kidnapped by men following orders from the Elector Frederick, Luther's friend and ruler of Saxony. The abduction had been planned secretly in Worms by Frederick, whom Aleander called "the fox." Luther remained at Wartburg for almost eleven months, where he translated the New Testament into German under the assumed name of Junker Georg. His whereabouts were kept secret for months. Even John, Frederick's own brother, didn't know where to find the reformer.[7]

In one of the most pivotal turnabouts in all church history, Frederick the Elector became God's means to keep Luther safe and to touch off what became the Protestant Reformation. The central doctrines of salvation by grace through faith alone and the sufficiency of Scripture alone as the Christian's rule of faith and practice were resurrected and safeguarded by the godly leaders of the Reformation.

52

He Also Delivers to Uzbekistan

UPS won't deliver to some remote places. Federal Express can't reach every spot on the globe. Even special couriers are prevented from entering certain locales. But God's Special Delivery service is hampered by no red tape, intimidated by no geographical barrier, disheartened by no earthly difficulty. He delivers on time, every time—in His time. Even when the obstacles seem insurmountable.

According to a 1991 article in *World* magazine, Olga Avetisova, a former ranking engineer in the building construction enterprise of Tashkent, Uzbekistan, supervised a ministry of mercy in the region's prisons, labor camps, and institutions.

The governor (or warden) of one of the prisons was antagonistic to Avetisova's ministry and refused to let her compassion workers inside. The director of the ministry requested prayer from supporting congregations, asking that God would open the way. They needed a special delivery if their work was to continue, so they dialed 1-800-SPECIAL DELIVERY. Remember the advertisement? "Call upon me in the day of trouble; I will deliver you, and you will honor me" (Psalm 50:15).

God's answer was quick and decisive: The governor was killed in a plane crash. Her successor promptly opened the gates to the church workers.

"We didn't pray for her to die," Avetisova insisted, "but just that the door would be opened."[8]

No Delivery Too Small or Too Large

Dr. Ed Goodrick taught Bible and theology at Multnomah School of the Bible for many years. He was a maverick if ever there was one, yet those who knew him also would insist that no one loved the Savior or His Word more than he. That was always true of him, even in his early days as a young pastor in Mossyrock, Washington.

Goodrick earnestly studied the Bible and preached it as best he understood it. He worked hard at making its truths come alive to his little congregation, and urged his parishioners to conform their lives to God's will. All his preaching and teaching centered on Scripture.

And that was just the problem for several upper-class members of the church. They wanted someone a little more, well, *refined*—someone who would teach the Bible less and discuss current events more.

A congregational meeting called to review Goodrick's performance was coming up and through the grapevine the pastor heard that a sizable and influential group within the church, led by the superintendent of the local school district, would call for his ouster. Goodrick had no interest in political maneuvering so he simply asked the elder board to judge him on whether his service met biblical standards. Then he committed the situation to God in prayer.

When the time for the congregational meeting arrived, Goodrick looked to be on his way out the door. On one side stood the superintendent and his party of influential and high-powered supporters. On the other was Goodrick and the church elders, most of whom were loggers ill-at-ease with such politicking.

When the moment arrived for Goodrick's review, the chairman of the board, Neil Kjesbu, stood up. Kjesbu possessed none of the sophistication or erudition of the anti-Goodrick faction—he was a simple stump farmer and part-time mailman—but his character had earned for him a powerful reputation in the community of six hundred. People liked Kjesbu and they respected him...probably more than anyone else in Mossyrock.

So when Kjesbu stood, gave Goodrick a glowing review, and expressed the hope that their pastor would be around for a good long time, the wind could be seen retreating from the superintendent's sails. In fact, he was almost speechless. "I don't know what you people think," he sputtered, "but as far as I am concerned, if our pastor is good enough for Neal Kjesbu, he's good enough for me!" With that, he sat and down and was silent for the rest of the meeting.[9]

Goodrick was quickly and overwhelmingly asked to stay on for another year, which ultimately turned into six. And God's Special Delivery service could add Pastor Ed Goodrick of Mossyrock to its long list of flabbergasted clients.

Pick Up the Phone and Call Now!

God's promise in Psalm 50:15 is addressed to all of His children. That includes you. The deal is simple: you're in trouble; you call out to Him; He delivers you; you give Him the glory. As Spurgeon said, it's a delightful partnership.

I could recite several more stories of God's Special Delivery service, such as the one about the Christian evangelist in Saudi Arabia who was dragged into Islamic Court and accused of lying about supernatural healings connected with his ministry. Being found guilty in a Muslim court brings horrifying consequences. Into the courtroom were marched thirty people suffering from various ailments. The prosecutor said, "If you are truly a man of God, then you will heal all of these people." Apparently that is just what happened, for sources say the evangelist was released and allowed to travel throughout the country without restrictions.[10]

Or I might mention how God is bringing to faith several former witch doctors in the nation of Uganda through His Special Delivery service. When a prime-time television broadcast showed feared witch doctor Patrick Kigozi burning his occult shrine, several other witch doctors decided to accept Christ. "If Jesus is so powerful that He can protect Patrick from the most powerful demons in Uganda," said Joyce Nakabugo, "then Jesus can protect me also."[11]

Such stories are thrilling, but I'd prefer not to continue recounting them. Because the real question now is not, "Does God operate a Special Delivery service?" but, "Do I believe He can deliver me?"

Do you? Do you believe the promise of Psalm 50:15?

Once again, I can't predict what form God's deliverance will take. I can't guess when He might knock at your door to make the delivery. He might appear tomorrow, He might wait for ten years. But I do know that He is the God of turnabouts and that He promises to deliver those who call on His name in faith.

So once again: do you believe in the God of turnabouts? Are you convinced that He keeps His word? Are you willing to stake your life on the hope that He always answers His 1-800-SPECIAL DELIVERY line?

If you're in trouble, call Him. Expect Him to deliver. And give Him the glory when the heavenly mailman arrives. Only then will you be able to agree with Spurgeon that the arrangement detailed in Psalm 50:15 is indeed a "delightful partnership."

Could that be a delivery van I see pulling up into your driveway?

Chapter 4

The Agony of Victory

*I*n 1913 American novelist Eleanor H. Porter created a fictional character who has been vilified ever since.

Porter's literary creation was a small girl who suffered innumerable trials but who steadfastly refused to acknowledge anything negative. She insisted on concerning herself only with the bright side of life.

One of my journalism professors, a curmudgeonly and sharp-tongued newspaperman, often used this character's name to reproach a student's work which he considered irritatingly optimistic. "I suppose next you'll tell me a good time was had by all," he'd sneer. And according to *Benet's Reader's Encyclopedia*, this character's name "has become a synonym for the fatuous, irrepressible optimist who always makes the best of things for himself and other people."[1]

So if critics ever walk up to you and say you remind them of Pollyanna, believe me, it's no compliment.

The problem with the Pollyannas of the world is that they don't seem familiar with this one. Looking for the bright side is commendable; but trying to calibrate your sundial at midnight is sheer lunacy.

It is preposterous to pretend that evil does not exist, that pain is illusory, and that everything you've always hoped for will be delivered to your door come sunrise. Life isn't like that. The hard truth is, people get hurt. They betray one another. They get sick, have accidents, say spiteful things, lose their jobs, cheat, steal, fail exams, are evicted from their homes, and die prematurely.

Even Christian people.

In this chapter I want to make it as clear as I can that belief in God's turnabouts is not some Pollyanna theology disconnected from the real world. I want to prevent readers from concluding that verses such as Psalm 50:15 and ideas like those in "Special Delivery" exempt them from the hardships common to humankind and the persecutions specific to believers. God's Special Delivery service runs on its own timetable and maintains its own code of business practices. It is certain God will deliver His people; it is seldom clear how or when He will do it.

Second, I want to insist that God performs some turnabouts even when He refuses to spare His people the slightest pain. I rejoice that most often God's turnabouts deflect Satan's fiery darts from reaching us. But sometimes God permits those flaming arrows to find their mark, *even as He continues to craft the turnabout.*

This is a hard idea for many of us to accept. We are so used to hearing about "the thrill of victory and the agony of defeat" that we forget that some triumphs hurt. There is such a thing as the agony of victory.

J. R. R. Tolkien in 1939 coined a term related to this idea. In a famous essay on fairy-stories (remember, Tolkien is the author of *The Hobbit* and *The Lord of the Rings* trilogy), he used the word *eucatastrophe* to describe a sudden turn of the story wherein darkness is turned to light and evil into good. But he insisted this "turn" in the story "is not essentially 'escapist' or 'fugitive.' In its fairy-tale—or-other-world—setting, it is a sudden and miraculous grace: never to be counted on to return." Further, this turn did not deny or make light of sorrow and failure, for their possibility "is necessary to the joy of deliverance," Tolkien said. What he did deny was a "universal final defeat."[2]

That's a good description of the agony of triumph. Not all turnabouts deliver God's people from great pain. Sometimes they do; at other times they don't. But in all cases, God is glorified. The turnabout proves that God rules from heaven and that at His word even the worst schemes of men and devils are reversed and made to proclaim His boundless splendor.

59

Hot and Bothered in Babylon

One of my favorite texts from the Old Testament is Daniel 3:16-18. The third chapter of Daniel tells the familiar story of three Hebrew captives—Shadrach, Meshach, and Abednego—who refused to worship King Nebuchadnezzar's golden statue and who were therefore tossed into a furnace heated seven times hotter than usual. Yet God spared their lives and used the incident to teach the king that even he, the greatest of all human potentates, amounted to less than a gnat in God's scheme of things. The chapter ends with a classic example of turnabout: "Then the king promoted Shadrach, Meshach and Abednego in the province of Babylon" (3:30). From toast to tops in one quick step.

The story has thrilled readers for millennia, but for our purposes I would like to focus on verses 16 through 18. I believe this passage offers tremendous clues on how to persevere whether God's turnabout spares us pain or not. There are reasons why God's servants were able to resist Nebuchadnezzar's demand that they bow before his idol:

> Shadrach, Meshach and Abednego replied to the king, "O Nebuchadnezzar, we do not need to defend ourselves before you in this matter. If we are thrown into the blazing furnace, the God we serve is able to save us from it, and he will rescue us from your hand, O king. But even if he does not, we want you to know, O king, that we will not serve your gods or worship the image of gold you have set up" (Daniel 3:16-18).

Note, first, that the three men stood together as one. "If *we* are thrown...the God *we* serve is able to save *us*..." etc. The Lone Ranger made a great childhood hero, but you will search in vain for him here. Tremendous power is offered us when we ally ourselves with others of like convictions.

Second, these were not Sunday Christians, part-time pew sitters, or theoretical theologians. Their faith was active, dynamic, and central to who they were: "...the God we *serve*..." Too many of us today hop from church to church, searching for the best menus and cooks to "feed" us. We have forgotten what it is to serve. If you want strength to persevere, it is far better to wait on tables than to pat your belly.

Third, these men knew the power of God. They were not blind—they could see for themselves Nebuchadnezzar's fierce demeanor, his ferocious troops, and his propensity for violence—yet their eyes were full of the might and grandeur of almighty God. "God...*is able to save us*..." They did not look for an Israeli commando unit to shoot up the place with

Uzis. They expected to see the omnipotent arm of God Himself.

Fourth, they knew God loved them with an everlasting love. It is one thing to understand that someone is strong; it is another to hope that he will use that strength on your behalf. These men held that expectation: "...and *he will rescue us* from your hand, O king..." They knew God well enough to expect a heavenly raiding party. But that is not all they knew.

Last, and most importantly, the three Hebrews recognized that God was God, and they weren't. They fully expected Him to deliver them; but they left room for God's sovereign choice: "But *even if he does not*, we want you to know, O king, that we will not serve your gods or worship the image of gold you have set up."

But even if he does not. Shadrach, Meshach, and Abednego served God faithfully together. They basked in His love and remained confident of His power. They expected to be players in a history-making turnabout. But they also knew that some of God's turnabouts called for stiff constitutions; and they resolved to stand firm, fire or freedom, death or deliverance, come what may. God would be glorified, "whether by life or by death" (*see* Philippians 1:20).

61

In this case, it was by life. Such is not always true, however.

Saws, Whips, and Chains

Some of the Christian faith's most celebrated heroes are listed in Hebrews 11. There you will read of Abel, Enoch, Noah, Abraham, Isaac and Jacob and Joseph and Moses and Rahab and many more. It is a ringing roll call of winners who "through faith conquered kingdoms, administered justice, and gained what was promised; who shut the mouths of lions, quenched the fury of the flames, and escaped the edge of the sword; whose weakness was turned to strength; and who became powerful in battle and routed foreign armies. Women received back their dead, raised to life again" (Hebrews 11:33-35a). The passage features more turnabouts per square inch than any other real estate in the Bible.

But did you notice where I *stopped* quoting?

Verse "35a" means the first half of the verse. The remainder of the text is just as inspired, just as profitable for our growth, just as glorifying to God. But the room chills considerably on the other side of the divider: "Others were tortured and refused to be released, so that they might gain a better resurrection. Some faced jeers and flogging, while still others were chained and put in prison. They were stoned; they were sawed in two; they were put to death by the sword. They went about in sheepskins and goatskins, destitute, persecuted and mistreated—the world was not worthy of them. They wandered in deserts and mountains, and in caves and holes in the ground" (11:35b-38).

Quite a different picture, isn't it? How many turnabouts did you count in *that* passage?

By the way, my question isn't meant to be rhetorical; I don't assume the answer "none." Why not? Because despite appearances, the second passage boasts almost as many turnabouts as the first. They're just wearing disguises.

If you were to track down the probable individuals alluded to in Hebrews 11:35b-38, you would run into people such as Micaiah (his turnabout is detailed in 1 Kings 22) and Jeremiah (Jeremiah 20) and Zechariah (2 Chronicles 24:17-27) and Elijah (2 Kings 1) and Isaiah (tradition says he was sawed in two) and even David (see chapter 6). All of these luminaries participated in one or more divine turn-abouts—and yet they themselves did not escape personal harm.

In the midst of some tremendous turnabouts, these godly men were hit by shrapnel. But if you asked them if the pain was worth it, all you'd hear is a chorus of "You bet!" (in Hebrew, of course). That's what I mean by the agony of victory.

They March in the Same Parade

In junior high and high school I marched in several parades as a member of the drum section. We were the ones responsible for helping the band to march together (which partially explains why it seldom did). Some parades are longer than others. The short ones are a piece of cake; the long ones make your stomach wish it had some. But while short parades appeal to musicians, long ones often score more points with the audience—especially if the show is spectacular. Floats and clowns and bands and antique cars and horses and beauty queens and sometimes even blimps can make for an unforgettable parade.

63

The parade of saints who know the agony of victory is a very long one. Their parade features God's breathtaking turnabouts one after another...each one different, each one surprising, yet each one unforgettable.

Part of the parade is even now winding its way through Communist China. In one area of Henan Province, a church of 260,000 believers has grown to about 600,000 in the last ten years. In Szechwan Province, where one of every forty people on earth live, nearly two thousand new churches have been planted in the past two to three years. Even the government recognizes the nation's mushrooming interest in the gospel. A September 1992 bulletin released by the

Beijing Statistical Bureau stated that 75 million Christians reside in China—triple the membership of the Communist Party.

Where the church just decades ago was thought to be all but wiped out, millions of Chinese are embracing Christ in an explosion of belief...and shrapnel has become a constant hazard.

In 1991 and 1992, according to one reporter, "local Communist authorities in some provinces began detaining, fining and beating Christians for their religious activities. In Henan Province, government officials made this decree: 'It was you Christians who brought down the regimes in Eastern Europe and the Soviet Union, but here in China we will stop you now!' "[3]

Communist authorities are making good on their threats, escalating raids on Christian meetings. Hundreds of foreign mission workers have been arrested, beaten, and jailed.

The authorities are trying their best to turn back the turnabout which has already taken place. Some of their tactics were revealed in Anhui Province, where devastating floods prompted believers to mount relief efforts for their brethren. Party functionaries moved quickly:

> With almost unbelievable callousness, Communist officials declared that flood victims who believe in Jesus are not to be given relief help. To the 20,000 affected Christians, the government message has been: "Tell them to go to their God for food and clothes."

> When Christians from Shanghai donated clothing for these fellow believers, they were promptly arrested, and their relief supplies were seized. When Anhui churches took up offerings from their own people to buy bread for both Christian and

non-Christian flood victims, the government accused the believers of trying to bribe people to convert, then confiscated the food and beat those involved.[4]

Still, the turnabout continues. David Wang, president of Asian Outreach, told of a woman whom authorities fined the equivalent of five years' wages for her Christian activities. When friends came to bail her out of jail, she demurred: "My mission is to minister the gospel to sinners," she said. "What better place for me to be?"[5]

This woman understands the agony of victory.

Breakthrough in Balangao

Another woman who is coming to understand the agony of victory is Joanne Shetler, the Wycliffe missionary we met in chapter 1. After living for years among the Balangaos, only two had put their trust in Christ. Shetler was heartsick. On a trip back to California to visit her home church, the weary missionary poured out her heart. Even her own "father," Ama, didn't believe—he and the rest of the tribe were too afraid of evil spirits. So Shetler's home church began praying, "God, show the Balangaos that you're stronger than the spirits. Make the Balangaos desire you; help them believe your Word."[6]

65

Shetler was anxious to see how God might answer that prayer, and equally eager to see the "miracle baby" who had been born in her absence. Andrea, one of the two Balangao believers, had prayed to be delivered from barrenness and Melisa was the answer. But Shetler discovered upon returning to Balangao that Melisa had died. She had been buried the day before. Shetler was terror-stricken.

No, No! my mind screamed. *Something is wrong.*

Surely God has made a mistake. Why, God? This baby can't die—she's an answer to our prayers! Why, God? Why?

I was sure that any possibility of Balangaos ever believing in God had just been demolished. What would happen to Andrea's faith?[7]

Andrea's faith never wavered. Balangaos grew up believing that the supernatural was all powerful and was not to be questioned. But the other villagers frightened Andrea when they suggested Melisa was in hell because she hadn't been baptized. Shetler showed Andrea from Scripture this was untrue, but the others had to be convinced. A local tradition demanded that everyone meet every night for nine nights after Melisa's burial to pray memorized prayers for her soul. Andrea asked the missionary to come and tell the people where Melisa was.

The Balangaos had a million questions. *Where did the dead go? What was it like there? Who is there? Does everyone go there?* Each night they asked more questions. *Where do we go when we die? What about the resurrection?* They grew so interested in the discussion that they insisted upon continuing their studies even after the nine days had expired. They began with the newly published Gospel of Mark.

And soon Shetler saw the turnabout, a victory touched with agony. Balangaos not only were listening to the gospel message; they were demanding to hear it. Shetler was flabbergasted:

How can one ever predict how God will bring himself glory? The heart-breaking, premature death of my friend's baby was God's avenue to answer my prayers, and the prayers of my friends back home in California.[8]

But Shetler still had more to learn of God's turnabouts. Some time later an incident similar to the Melisa episode occurred.

Shetler had seen God defeat the evil spirits of Balangao so dramatically and often that she says "we came to expect the miraculous. That's why I wasn't afraid when they came running to me with Baltazar's little boy who was unconscious." A turnabout was in the making—but it would be touched with agony:

> The child had been with his granddaddy, who was a spirit medium. The old man was sacrificing a pig when this little boy, not quite six years old, cut off one of its ears and was playing with it. The spirits spoke through the grandfather: they wanted that ear back. But the boy wouldn't give it to them. So, the spirits said they'd just take the boy, and he fell over unconscious.[9]

The parents were terrified; no sacrifice existed to atone for defying the spirits. They scooped up the boy and took him to Shetler's house. She sent for the church elders and they prayed. Finally they took the lad home. But soon thereafter she heard the death wail—the boy had died.

67

> *No! No!* My mind was screaming. *What has happened? What went wrong? Why did he die? This isn't working. God, you've made a mistake. Now people will just stop believing.*[10]

Shetler was crushed. But believers surrounded Baltazar's grieving family day and night and "the comfort and reality of God were irresistible. A week later the entire family of that little boy became believers. I was dumbfounded.... I simply had to resign as the manager of God's glory."[11]

Friends, the plain truth is, none of us is qualified to manage God's glory. None of us is wise enough, godly enough, mature enough, or even imaginative enough to predict how, when, where, or why God will bring glory to His name.

Elisabeth Elliot skillfully pointed this out in *Through Gates of Splendor*, an account of the events leading up to January 8, 1956, the day five young missionaries (including Elliot's husband, Jim) would be speared to death trying to bring the gospel to a savage tribe of South American Indians called the Aucas. Nearly three years after this tragedy, Elliot found herself within ten feet of one of the seven men who killed her husband. She and her three-and-a-half-year-old daughter had returned to the Aucas' territory to point these men to the Lord. And they were listening.

"How did this come to be?" Elliot asked. "Only God who made iron swim, who caused the sun to stand still, in whose hand is the breath of every living thing—only this God, who is our God forever and ever, could have done it."[12] She wrote that the Aucas told them their attack was a mistake; they thought the white men were cannibals and they now regarded the killings as an error. Elliot, however, saw it another way:

> But we know that it was no accident. God performs all things according to the counsel of His own will. The real issues at stake on January 8, 1956, were very far greater than those which immediately involved five young men and their families, or this small tribe of naked "savages."[13]

> God is the God of human history, and He is at work continuously, mysteriously, accomplishing His eternal purposes in us, through us, for us, and in spite of us.[14]

68

I think that's another way of saying that turnabout is God's play, and that there is such a thing as the agony of victory. John Hus might well agree.

Snapshot from an Old Parade

The saints who have marched in the agony of victory are part of a long parade, but it's also a very old one. It stretches all the way across the world and from this moment in time to the distant past. Do you recall Martin Luther from the last chapter? He was marching in this parade before God yanked him from his place so he could sign for a Special Delivery. To that point, Martin had been striding shoulder to shoulder with a man named John Hus. John never received a Special Delivery, however; he kept on marching to the end. His end.

John Hus lived almost exactly a century before Martin Luther. He was a popular preacher in his native Bohemia (roughly equivalent to the former Czechoslovakia) and "raised the curtain on the Reformation on the Continent, adopting Wycliffe's theology and anticipating many of the 16th century Reformers' key ideas."[15] He scathingly criticized the pope's sale of indulgences to raise cash for a 1412 crusade against the king of Naples—the pope promised full remission of sins to anyone who supported Rome[16]—and agreed with Wycliffe that the invisible church of the elect took precedence over the institutional, hierarchical organization. Both positions threatened the pope's authority and put Hus on a fast track to the stake. He was excommunicated in 1410 by the archbishop of Prague and by Rome in 1412.

In 1414, the Council of Constance convened to heal "the Great Schism" (in which rival popes ruled from different cities), sort out the church's problems in Bohemia, and

69

effect some long-overdue reforms. The emperor Sigismund invited Hus to attend and promised him safe conduct in both directions. Despite some hesitations, Hus decided to go. But within a month he was seized by followers of Pope John XXII and imprisoned. He was tried by the council and proclaimed a heretic on July 6, 1415. Then he was taken to the outskirts of the city, tied to a stake by a chain around his neck, and burned to death. According to *Foxe's Book of Martyrs*, at the stake Hus refused one last offer to recant, saying, "What error should I renounce, when I know myself guilty of none? For this was the principal end and purpose of my doctrine, that I might teach all men repentance and remission of sins, according to the verity of the Gospel of Jesus Christ: wherefore, with a cheerful mind and courage, I am here ready to suffer death."[17]

As the fire crackled around his body, Hus began to sing loudly to Christ. He died a martyr to the cause of Jesus and his ashes were cast into the river Rhine so the least memory of the man might be erased.

But it was not erased. In fact, the burning of Hus ignited a fire that would burst into full flame one hundred years later in a sleepy German town called Wittenberg. Hus never saw the completion of the turnabout he initiated, but he was an integral part of it nonetheless. He marched in the Agony of Victory parade and was welcomed home with as big a ticker-tape celebration as Martin Luther would ever enjoy.

Two godly men, two separate destinies. Luther received a Special Delivery; Hus was awarded the Agony of Victory. Yet both well represented the Father of Lights, Luther by igniting the Reformation and Hus by illuminating his countrymen with the sacrifice of himself. And the God of turnabouts received great glory through both men.

Four Verses from the End

I doubt whether this chapter brought you as much comfort as the previous one was designed to. I know I didn't have nearly as much fun writing it. Who likes pain and suffering? Those who do we call masochists, and they aren't listed in any concordance I know of.

All concordances *do* list the term "suffering," however. Several times. And while the Scriptures never lift up suffering as a biblical goal, it is a biblical given. Consider Philippians 1:29: "For it has been granted to you on behalf of Christ not only to believe on him, but also to suffer for him." Those same concordances will also point you to some version of Colossians 1:28-29:

> We proclaim him [Christ], admonishing and teaching everyone with all wisdom, so that we may present everyone perfect in Christ. To this end I labor, struggling with all his energy, which so powerfully works in me.

This Colossians passage accurately describes the parade we've been watching throughout this chapter. In verse 28 Paul described the *victory* he worked so hard to achieve: "That we may present everyone perfect in Christ." What a triumph! What an ending! What a grand finale to a glorious parade! But the apostle knew he wouldn't reach the end of the march without some *agony*—in fact, the word translated "struggling" in verse 29 comes from the Greek term *agonizomai*, which eventually dropped into the English language as the word "agony."

Paul not only taught this stuff, he lived it. I won't take time now to review how deeply he lived it, but I do want to call final attention to the words you'll find four verses from the end of his life.

71

The apostle's final instruction to his contemporaries and to us is found in 2 Timothy. This would be his last book before the Romans would cut short his days. Apparently he already felt the cold steel of the executioner's sword on his neck, for in 4:6 he wrote, "I am already being poured out like a drink offering, and the time has come for my departure."

He had fought the good fight; he had finished the race; he had kept the faith. He knew the end was near and that, this time, he could expect no Special Delivery.

And yet, somehow, four verses from the end of his last book he has the chutzpah to write:

> The Lord will rescue me from every evil attack and will bring me safely to his heavenly kingdom. To him be glory for ever and ever. Amen (4:18).

Now, it seems to me that execution by beheading should qualify for "an evil attack." I surely wouldn't put it in the "friendly greeting" category, would you? What's up here, anyway? We already saw that Paul knew he was about to die. It's even likely he could guess the means. So how could he say "the Lord will rescue me from every evil attack"?

I think he could say it because he believed with all his heart in the agony of victory.

He saw down the corridor of time and was struck speechless at the final turnabout he witnessed God preparing. His mind boggled at how all the solitary turnabouts throughout history were being woven by divine cunning into a stupendous, heart-stopping mother of all turnabouts at the return of Christ. He insisted that although evil could touch him (when permitted), it could not ultimately hurt him. And he believed in *eucatastrophe*, a sudden turn of the story wherein darkness is turned to light and evil into good, where sorrow or failure is never denied but where a universal final defeat is.

That is, he believed in the God of turnabouts.

So what sword that delivered him into his loving Father's arms could be called "evil"? The man who brandished the blade might give it such a name, but not the one who joyfully leapt from earth to heaven.

That is the agony of victory. There might be weeping in the night, but laughter greets the morning.

Your morning, too. I don't deny your tears. I don't make light of your pain. But I *do* know that if you're marching in this parade right now, one of the most important issues in your life should be a good understanding of English grammar. Word order is crucial in our language. And in this parade, it's paramount. Don't miss the sequence. Even though agony pushes its nose somewhere up toward the front, it's another three-syllable word that blows the final trumpet blast.

Vic - to - ry. And it's all yours.

Chapter 5

Speedy Gonzales, Theologian

"Ándale, ándale, arriba, arriba, YEEEHA!"

I'm not sure that he was the primary one responsible for getting me started on a ten-year-long study of Spanish, but I know he was at least a big early influence. How could you watch Speedy Gonzales on a bright Saturday morning and not wish he could be your friend?

Speedy was one cool mouse. You can keep your Mighty Mouses, your Jerries (of Tom and), even your Mickeys and Minnies. For me, there was but one radical rodent: Speedy Gonzales, speed demon, heartthrob, and a cat's worst nightmare.

Speedy was *fast*. Like lightning. Like a rocket. Like the U.S.S. *Enterprise* at warp 9. I mean, the little guy could cruise. Just when his feline foes thought they had him trapped, *Zip!*, he'd not only escape their claws but relieve them of their shorts. That was why all the *señorita* mice thought only of *amor* whenever Speedy passed their way.

"If that mouse speaks Spanish," I'd say to myself, "then I want to, too."

It's been years since I've seen Speedy scorch up the screen, but I still think of him fondly. I've even come to regard him more highly than I did in my prepubescent years. Today I consider him not only a dashing hero, but a pretty nifty theologian.

Light Speed Theology

Speedy has come to represent for me one of the most delightful species of God's turnabouts. Just when Satan appears ready to snag us in his wicked clutches, *Zip!*, God blasts in at light speed and not only rescues us but leaves the Devil shivering in his BVDs.

This kind of turnabout is *fast*, like a champion roper at the rodeo. No sooner does the bull burst from the Devil's holding pen than it is roped, hog-tied, and left squirming on the arena floor to the furious applause of a delighted audience.

This kind of turnabout appeals to us for many reasons. We like the idea that our dreadful circumstances won't menace us for long. We take courage at the thought that a fearsome storm front is about to dissipate in an onslaught of balmy weather. We delight in seeing God work *fast*.

And the encouraging thing is, God seems to get a kick out of it, too.

I know this not only because we can watch Him at work, but because He openly talks about it. Much of our biblical information about turnabouts comes from observing the way God works with His people. But in this instance, He's anxious to describe for us what He loves to do. Consider Isaiah 42 as one example.

The prophet begins with a famous description of the coming Messiah, one of the several "Servant Songs" featured in the book. Beginning with verse 10, the chapter shifts focus to the appropriate response expected of both Israel and the world. The Lord is glorious and so is His Messiah—so give them the praise they deserve! Then Isaiah's vision moves to God Himself and what He is about to do:

> The LORD will march out like a mighty man,
>> like a warrior he will stir up his zeal;
> with a shout he will raise the battle cry
>> and will triumph over his enemies
>>> (Isaiah 42:13).

Then it's time to hear from the Holy One of Israel Himself, who delights in describing His war plans on behalf of His people:

> For a long time I have kept silent,
>> I have been quiet and held myself back.
> *But now, like a woman in childbirth,*
>> *I cry out, I gasp and pant.*
> I will lay waste the mountains and hills
>> and dry up all their vegetation;
> I will turn rivers into islands
>> and dry up the pools.
> I will lead the blind by ways they have not known,
>> along unfamiliar paths I will guide them;
> I will turn the darkness into light before them
>> and make the rough places smooth.
> These are the things I will do;
>> I will not forsake them
>>> (Isaiah 42:14-16, italics mine).

77

It is an earthshaking description of a divine turnabout. Darkness is transformed to light. The rough places are made smooth. Rivers are swallowed and mountains get blasted into plains. But notice that all this seismic activity happens *suddenly*, like a woman giving birth. Things had been quiet for nine months; but in the middle of the night the baby decides he's waited long enough.

Don't get caught up in the welter of images connected with a delivery room. The point isn't that God is in pain or that labor might take several agonizing hours. The force of this picturesque language is that oftentimes when God is ready to unveil a turnabout, He does it with blinding speed: "For a long time I have kept silent, I have been quiet and held myself back. *But now…*"

It's the Speedy Gonzales syndrome:

> Lickety split,
> just that quick,
> the Devil's behind
> gets a kick.

This is a common theme in Isaiah. Six chapters later the Lord is rebuking the nation Israel for her ungodliness and He sees the need to remind the people Who they are supposed to be serving:

> I foretold the former things long ago,
> my mouth announced them and I made them
> known;
> *then suddenly I acted,*
> and they came to pass
> (Isaiah 48:3, italics mine).

The Lord not only knows the end from the beginning, He creates both of them (as well as everything in between!). He frequently acts with blinding speed and in dramatic ways to remind us that He rules the world with an iron scepter. Beings bound by time—such as you and me—are

78

impressed with great power compressed into tiny blips. That's one reason why Speedy Gonzales makes such a fine theologian: not only is his content good, but his delivery is outstanding.

Surprise in the Solomons

One astonishing example of a speedy turnabout was reported recently in the mountain districts of the Solomon Islands in the Coral Sea close by Australia.[1]

Field evangelists with Every Home for Christ decided to venture into the territory of the twenty thousand-member Koios tribe, even though tribe members had earlier murdered a British government official and three Catholic priests. After spending a week praying and fasting, EHFC workers approached a Koio village. Immediately they were seized and brought before six tribal elders who sat outside the quarters of their gravely ill high chief. "The workers soon concluded they would never be able to share the gospel with the Koio people without the chief's blessing," said the article detailing this incident. But God was about to turn darkness into light, level mountains into plains, and dry up raging rivers.

Unexpectedly, the tribal leaders decided to permit the missionaries to meet their chief and speak with him. Team members were led into the chief's private bedroom and soon came face to face with a frail old man lying in a traditional "earth bed," a hollow dug out of the ground. The missionaries were astonished when the chief not only gave them his full attention, but recited a prayer asking the Lord Jesus to become his Savior. That done, *he breathed his last and died.*

It's important to remember at this point that a turnabout requires that the skies must first turn dark and threatening.

In this case, the heavens opened and a monsoon poured down.

As the villagers realized what had happened, their interest in the newcomers turned from curiosity to fury. The white men had not healed their chief, but killed him! Tension immediately rose by a factor of ten...and the evangelists prayed as never before. They were in need of a turnabout, and quickly.

They got one.

> With the lives of the young evangelists hanging in the balance, a second miracle occurred. The old chief suddenly revived and sat straight up in bed. The villagers were awestruck when he called for 60 close friends and family members to gather for a special meeting. As they crowded around him, the old man related a vivid account of what he had seen in the previous hours—an amazing story of heaven and hell, angels and Jesus.

80

> "I have returned," the chief told his astonished people, "to tell you that we must stop worshiping false gods, and that we must listen to the message these men have brought to our village." After admonishing the workers to continue their witness, the Koio's chief quietly passed away for good.[2]

The chief returned to this world for only two hours, but it was long enough for God to complete His turnabout. All six village elders made commitments to Christ within minutes of their leader's death. As news of the incident spread throughout the Koio's territory, nine churches and thirty-six smaller fellowships quickly were established—all in an area without any gospel witness prior to mid-1990. As of today, almost four thousand Koios have professed faith in Christ, including a group of three hundred believers from the deceased chief's village.

Faster than a Speeding Bullet

The old TV show "Superman" claimed its hero was faster than a speeding bullet, but some of God's turnabouts make the big "S" look like an arthritic tortoise.

Ron and Beth Koopman, missionaries to Venezuela from my boyhood church, had returned home on furlough. One sunny day one of their daughters was playing outside when, as children will do, Kim decided to dash across the street. She forgot her parents' stern warnings to look both ways before venturing from the sidewalk and instead bolted out into the middle of the road, heedless of whatever traffic might be heading her way.

From inside the house, Beth saw the whole terrible scene unfold in nightmarish slow motion: her daughter dashing into the street directly in the path of an oncoming car, the vehicle unable to screech to a halt in time. In an instant, Beth's heart told her the truth. Her thirty-pound daughter could not win a contest with a two thousand-pound car moving at twenty-five miles per hour.

81

Beth couldn't look. She turned away in a flood of tears.

Seconds later a neighbor burst into the house, weeping that she had seen the whole thing. "I'm sorry, I'm so sorry," she cried.

Just then Beth looked up...and *saw her daughter in one piece on the other side of the road.* It was impossible! There had not been enough time for her even to lurch back to her starting place, much less beat the car and run to the other side. And yet, there she was. Without a scratch.

The neighbor was flabbergasted. So was the driver, who swore he heard the thump of an impact. Both thought they

saw the girl get hit. At first Beth could not imagine what
had happened, but later concluded there could be but one
answer: Psalm 91:11-12:

> For he will command his angels concerning you
>> to guard you in all your ways;
> they will lift you up in their hands,
>> so that you will not strike your foot
>> against a stone.

Or against a bumper, apparently. Angelic intervention
seemed to be the only explanation for what transpired that
day; nothing else fit. The simple fact was that the laws of
physics had been violated. Kim could not possibly have
ended up where she did, yet there she was. And nobody saw
how she got there—even eyewitnesses thought they saw
something else.

Speedy Gonzales would have smiled. He knows a *pron-
to* turnabout when he sees one.

And this incident truly could be termed a turnabout. Not
only was the Koopman's daughter spared physical harm, but
her divine rescue immeasurably increased the family's faith
in the goodness and providence of God. A horrific tragedy
was transformed into a joyful occasion to celebrate the God
of life-saving reversals.

Oops! into *Wow!*

As any fan of Speedy could tell you, many instant turn-
arounds are more hilarious than dramatic. Rebecca Manley
Pippert knows whereof I speak.

In her excellent book on friendship evangelism, *Out of
the Saltshaker and into the World*, Becky tells how she was
invited as part of a team to teach for a week at Stanford
University on the topic of evangelism. While there she met

82

Lois—bright, sensitive, and skeptical about the existence of God. After several conversations, Becky invited her to a Bible study in a dorm room. "Okay, I'll come," Lois responded. "But the Bible won't have anything relevant to say to me."[3]

The next day Becky discovered Lois was living off campus with her boyfriend, Phil. He decided to join her at the study. Without knowing Lois's background, Becky had chosen John 4 as the study text, a passage about a woman with multiple sexual partners. It was then that Becky began to sweat:

> I began introducing the chapter to the group, noticed Phil and Lois sitting there, and suddenly remembered the passage dealt with a woman who had sexual problems. I feared Lois would think I had planned this just for her.
>
> With a step of faith, I frantically tried to think of how to avoid the crunch of the passage (though I was sure God had got me into this mess). Lois and Phil were seated close to my left. Thinking it would be better if Lois did not read the passage aloud, I called on Sally, who was immediately to my right, calculating that if each person read a paragraph aloud, we would finish before it was Lois's turn.
>
> To my dismay a girl three seats away from Lois started reading. (I discovered later it was Sally's twin sister who happened to be sitting next to me.) Then Lois read the portion: "Jesus said to her, 'You are right in saying, "I have no husband"...for the man you're living with now is not your husband.' " It was her first experience of reading Scripture and her eyes grew as big as saucers, while I hid behind my Bible!

83

"I must say, this is a bit more relevant than I had expected," she commented with considerable under-statement.[4]

This comical turnabout began with an outmaneuvered Bible study leader and would conclude the next day when Lois saw the truth of the gospel and committed her life to Christ. Or did it really conclude then? Perhaps not. Lois immediately moved out of her apartment with Phil, a choice which infuriated him and prompted three other girls to get right with Jesus. The next day school officials told Lois she could move into a dorm, unheard of at such a late date, and her roommate turned out to be a dynamic, mature Christian. "Wow, what a turnabout!" you say. Yes, but it still wasn't finished. Three months later Phil became a Christian. After his conversion he told his former lover, "Thanks, Lois, for loving God enough to put him first instead of me. Your obedience affected my eternal destiny."[5]

Ah, the sweet exhilaration of serving a God who delights in full-throttle turnabouts! Almost before you have time to get worried, He zips in and exchanges gloom for glory. And not just on the mission field or in evangelistic encounters! Speedy raced around all kinds of neighbor-hoods. So does God.

From Out of the Blue

I had been discipling a young man for about a year when he approached me with a thorny problem. He wanted to set something right which had gone wrong many years before, and he wanted my advice on how to do it. But once I heard the particulars of his dilemma, I quickly knew it was over my head. By about twenty miles.

My friend had not become a Christian until a few years after his college graduation. While in school he immersed himself in many of the things that infatuate so many college students: drinking, experimenting with drugs, promiscuity. One of his illicit sexual liaisons produced an unwanted pregnancy. He had no interest in marrying the girl and so arranged to pay for an abortion. The "romance" soured almost immediately and the relationship suffered a nasty breakup. Both parties went their separate ways, and not as friends.

Years later, once he began learning and practicing a biblical lifestyle, my friend became convinced he should somehow get in touch with this former girlfriend, ask her forgiveness, and tell her he had become a Christian. But several problems stood in the way. First, the incident had transpired six or seven years prior to his conversion and he had no idea where the girl lived. They had not contacted each other since the breakup. Second, he was married now and was apprehensive that if he tried to locate the girl and communicate with her, she might interpret it as an attempt to renew their affair. Third, he feared that by contacting her he might inadvertently open some very rancid and painful sores that would be excruciating to close. But he insisted on doing something; he felt God prompting him to take action. But what?

"Steve, you've been a Christian for a long time," he said to me. "What do *you* think I should do?"

I immediately thought of Solomon's predicament described in 1 Kings 3:16-28. His dilemma called for extraordinary wisdom, and Solomon delivered—so much so that "when all Israel heard the verdict the king had given, they held the king in awe, because they saw that he had wisdom from God to administer justice" (1 Kings 3:28). The problem was, about the only thing Solomon and I had in common were the letters bracketing our first names. I had no clue what to tell my friend. But I did come up with what I

85

thought was sage, well-reasoned advice. My counsel not only seemed wise, I felt pretty humble about it—even if I did think so myself.

"Boy, this is out of my league," I said, shaking my head. "But I'll tell you what. The pastor is out of town right now, but he's due back in about five days. Why don't you give him a call, set up an appointment, and ask him? He's probably dealt with cases like this before. He'd know a lot better than I would about what you should do."

There, it was said. In one magnanimous speech I had been humble, I had commended my pastor, and I had been wise—not in Solomon's category, perhaps, but serviceable.

Ha!

It never entered my mind what God would do next. The following day I got a phone call from my excited friend.

"Steve, you'll never guess what happened," he said.

"You're right," I replied, "I won't. What's up?"

"My wife and I were sitting at home yesterday afternoon and the phone rang. Guess who it was?"

"I have no idea."

"It was my old girlfriend—the one I got pregnant! She just called from out of the blue—no particular reason, no agenda. I yelled to my wife and we both got on the phone. I told her I had become a Christian and asked her to forgive me for what we had done. She did. We talked for a few minutes and then she hung up. What do you think of that?"

If only he knew.

My first thought concerned the density of my pea brain. My second scoffed at my sham humility. It wasn't until my third thought that I began to laugh at the wonder and unpredictability of the plan of God.

I thought I had been wise in suggesting that my friend wait for several days before doing anything. Meanwhile,

God put on His Nikes and tore up the track accomplishing
what I could never have imagined. I had hoped for a nice
little turnabout, say, in a few weeks or months; God decided
to dazzle a young Christian with His Speedy Gonzales imi-
tation. (No, that's not true. God is the original, Speedy the
replica. Come to think of it, Speedy's not even real. He's
some artist's idea of a jet-powered mouse who speaks
Spanish. Sheesh. Discussions like this make it easy to see
what I meant about my pea brain, don't they?)

That's the way it is with some of God's turnabouts.
You're in the soup, the burner's about to be turned up to
"high," and suddenly you're not in the soup, you're eating
it. And loving every moment of the whole delicious meal.

Speedy Stares in Awe

Glorious thoughts of such magnificent turnabouts filled
Isaiah's mind. You can't wander far in his book without
bumping into some version of this idea. But I think one of
my favorites appears at the end of one late chapter, shining
like a diamond in the noonday sun.

Isaiah has just described a future when Israel would be
regathered to her land in righteousness. The chapter glows
with one brilliant promise after another, painting a scene of
breathtaking beauty and awesome possibilities. "The least
of you will become a thousand," Isaiah enthuses, "the
smallest a mighty nation." But he saves the best for last.
You almost wonder if Isaiah had a vision of Speedy
Gonzales somewhere in his prophetic ministry. The final
sentence of Isaiah 60 could well serve as the starting gun on
the race track of God's speediest turnabouts:

> I am the LORD;
>> in its time I will do this swiftly
>>> (Isaiah 60:22b).

On your marks, get set...oops, the race is already over. God wins! Again!

"Andale, ándale, arriba, arriba, YEEEHA!"

Chapter 6

*Molasses Is Slow,
But It's Still Sweet*

*B*ack in 1986 an aged man walked painfully to the front of Western Seminary's chapel, took a seat, and in a thick accent heavy with emotion began to recount story after story of God's providence in the midst of unspeakable horror.

"My very, very dear children," he began, "I know you are at an age when you don't like to be called children. But I call you children, not in order to demean you, but because in a very real sense of the word, you *are* my children.... I prayed for you, when you were babes. When we were in communist jails, in cells thirty feet beneath the earth...every night, other prisoners and I would kneel and would pray for America, for its churches, and for its children.... You are children of the persecuted church which prayed for America."

Richard Wurmbrand, the Romanian pastor who authored *Tortured for Christ*, held us spellbound for almost an hour. He apologized for having to sit while speaking to us, but explained that fourteen years of beatings had taken its toll on his feet. He could no longer stand in place for more than a few moments.

He told how he and his comrades had languished—forgotten, they thought—in gray, underground cells illuminated by a single naked light bulb dangling from the bare ceiling. He recalled how their years of imprisonment sponged away the memory of colors, how they had forgotten the voices and sometimes the faces of loved ones, how they longed to see the carefree faces of little children.

He described the mildest of the indignities inflicted on them by their communist torturers. "They did worse things than that," he said after his listeners gaped in disbelief, "I will not say more."

But through all the terror, he focused on just one thing: his great, majestic God, the High and Holy One, who sustained them through the interminable years of darkness. There was no bitterness, no desire to be lifted up as a stellar example of courageous faith. Just a simple man who loved his Savior and who hoped that, someday, his country and his captors might come to that same faith. But back in 1986, there seemed little hope of that.

I heard nothing more of Pastor Wurmbrand until last year. I discovered that he had been asked to return to Romania to visit his Christian countrymen once the Iron Curtain began to rust into dust. In one city a Christian bookstore had been opened—the first one in memory—and he was asked if he would like to see the warehouse. He did, and was led down some stairs into a small room stuffed with books.

Wurmbrand took one look, froze in surprise, spun around, and took his wife into his arms. Then in full view of all present, this elderly saint whose battered feet require him to sit while lecturing began to dance with joy.

The warehouse was his old cell.

God had performed a stunning turnabout. In the very room where one believer formerly was tortured, many were now being fed spiritually. Where Satan once did his best to destroy the church, God was building it up.

Heaven had engineered a flip-flop of gargantuan proportions...but took many years and countless tears to accomplish it.

Slow Doesn't Mean Apathetic

When God through the apostle Peter says that "with the Lord a day is like a thousand years, and a thousand years are like a day" (2 Peter 3:8), He meant to remind us that His Daytimer is markedly different from ours. We get impatient when we have to wait three minutes for microwave popcorn; He's content to spend decades in conforming us to the image of Christ. His "slowness" in working out the details of our lives—even in delivering a turnabout we desperately need—doesn't mean He doesn't care. It just might mean His Daytimer is open to five years from now, while we're focused on tomorrow.

There are scores of biblical examples to prove the point. God promised aged Abraham a son—and then made him wait a quarter of a century before He gave him one. He allowed Israel to spend over four hundred years in Egyptian captivity before He brought about one of the greatest turnabouts of all time. Jesus told us He would return to set this world aright—and we've been waiting two thousand years to see it happen.

The fact is, God performs some of His turnabouts s-l-o-w-l-y. He takes weeks, months, years, decades, centuries, even millennia to turn a satanic shuttle to Sheol into a highway to heaven.

But He is still the God of turnabouts!

Perhaps one of the best biblical examples of this is the life of King David. Or perhaps I should say, David who *eventually* became king. You'll see the significance of my distinction in a moment.

Turnabout over Time

We first meet David in 1 Samuel 16. Saul, the first king of Israel, had just committed the grievous sin that stirred the prophet Samuel to thunder, "Because you have rejected the word of the LORD, he has rejected you as king" (1 Samuel 15:23). God then sent Samuel to Bethlehem to choose another king for the nation. Samuel arrives at the household of Jesse and is introduced to seven of Jesse's sons, but none of them are the Lord's choice for Israel's new king. "Are these all the sons you have?" asks Samuel of Jesse.

"There is still the youngest," Jesse answers, "but he is tending the sheep."

"Send for him," says Samuel, "we will not sit down until he arrives" (1 Samuel 16:10-11). The text then says:

So he sent and had him brought in. He was ruddy, with a fine appearance and handsome features.

Then the Lord said, "Rise and anoint him; he is the one."

So Samuel took the horn of oil and anointed him in the presence of his brothers, and from that day on the Spirit of the Lord came upon David in power (16:12-13).

Note carefully David's circumstances. He is the youngest of eight boys, a young teen at most. His father did not think it worthwhile to schedule him for an interview about the royal job opening. He comes in from the fields stinking of sheep...and God says, "Rise and anoint him; he is the one."

What a turnabout! From neglected, smelly little brother, to king, in one swift reversal.

Or...maybe not so swift.

True, David had been anointed king of Israel by one of the nation's greatest prophets. But his head wouldn't feel the weight of a crown for ages. In fact, before David finally sat on the throne a few life experiences would be his to enjoy:

> He survived at least nine murder attempts by Saul.
> He was forced to flee for his life and feign insanity.
> He lived as an outlaw in caves and became an attraction for "all those who were in distress or in debt or discontented" (1 Samuel 22:2).
> He twice spared Saul's life when he could have killed him.
> He married several women and fathered several children.
> He became an expert raider and a deadly guerrilla fighter.

93

At long last, David became king—but only king of Judah (2 Samuel 2:4). Saul's son, Ish-Bosheth, still ruled over Israel. A war broke out between David's supporters and those of Ish-Bosheth, and Scripture says "the war between the house of Saul and the house of David lasted a long time" (2 Samuel 3:1). It wasn't until David reached his thirtieth birthday that hostilities ceased and he became the king he was anointed to be many weary years before on his father's peaceful estate (2 Samuel 5:3-4).

When David at last sat on the throne of a unified Israel, God had completed His promised turnabout. *But He did it in His own time.*

It may be that you are in desperate need of a turnabout. If your circumstances don't change, you see no hope for the future. Just a few days ago at a weekend retreat I spoke to one young man who feels exactly this way. He can't understand why God seems to have placed his life "on hold."

What do you do if you find yourself in a divine holding pattern? What do you do should you be caught in a long struggle between the forces of light and the forces of darkness? What do you do? There's probably no one better to ask than David himself. His potent prescription is found in Psalm 131:

> My heart is not proud, O LORD,
>   my eyes are not haughty;
> I do not concern myself with great matters
>   or things too wonderful for me.
> But I have stilled and quieted my soul;
>   like a weaned child with its mother,
>   like a weaned child is my soul within me.
> O Israel, put your hope in the LORD
>   both now and forevermore.

Israel's ancient advice columnist urged his impatient readers to follow a three-step course of action:

1. Remember who you are. You are not God. You do not know the end from the beginning nor can you guess how things will ultimately turn out. "Each day has enough trouble of its own," said Jesus in Matthew 6:34, so do not concern yourself with how things *might* unfold; those are things "too wonderful" for us. Experts say that more than ninety percent of the things we worry about never happen, so leave the future where it belongs: in God's very capable hands.

2. Snuggle up against God's chest. Get as near to Him as you possibly can, and quiet your heart. David knew this doesn't happen by accident; he said "*I have stilled* and quieted my soul." He had to consciously downshift because he knew he wouldn't do it naturally. As a father, David remembered that a weaned child does not fuss and yammer and whine as it did before it grew out of that stage. It is simply content to be near its mother—and that is how he wanted to be in the presence of almighty God.

3. Never give up hope. At the proper time, God will act in the most flabbergasting ways for your benefit. The word "hope" implies that something good is out there in the future, just waiting to smother you in a king-sized grizzly bear hug. You don't know its shape or its size or even its E.T.A., but it's out there. In fact, if you knew any of those details, your hope wouldn't be the genuine article. Paul reminds us that "hope that is seen is no hope at all. Who hopes for what he already has? But if we hope for what we do not yet have, we wait for it patiently" (Romans 8:24-25). It's always too soon to give up on God.

95

Are you anxious about some excruciating situation that just doesn't seem to change? Are you worried that God seems to be moving too slowly for your tastes? If so, remember that it's very possible God may be setting the stage for the turnabout you so desperately need. So don't give up if it takes awhile to materialize! Some of God's turnabouts—whether we like it or not—take years to fully develop.

But When They Do Appear—Oh, My!

Mongolia has traditionally been at the bottom of every statistical category related to church growth in Asia. European missionaries worked there until the 1930s, but the first known Mongol converts weren't recorded until the early 1980s.

With the massive changes now rocking Eastern Europe, however, things have changed. Missionaries have poured into the country, armed with tracts, Scriptures, and even Campus Crusade for Christ's film, *Jesus*. A Christian radio program debuted on the state-controlled network last November.

And what has been the outcome? A turnabout of almost unimaginable proportions:

> The result of these efforts has been a whopping, 3,000 percent increase in the size of the Mongol church over the past two years. Fellowships have been planted in the capital of Ulan Bator, and urban nationals are readying plans to take the gospel into the nation's hinterlands.[1]

God is on the march across the globe, turning citadels of the Evil One into Pony Express stations for the gospel. And nowhere is the turnabout more astonishing than in the former Soviet Union.

96

A Russian Reversal

It may not have been clear to many of us, but God has been spending part of His time in the last seventy-five years preparing to unveil a turnabout of global proportions. The Soviet Union—an officially atheistic state which former U.S. president Ronald Reagan called "the Evil Empire"—is now one of the most fertile mission fields in the world.

Philip Yancey and eighteen other evangelicals were invited in late 1991 to visit the Soviet Union in order to discuss how American Christians might help the struggling nation. The most startling thing about the invitation was its author: the chairman and four other members of the Supreme Soviet. Yancey was at first skeptical, but by the end of his visit came away convinced that he had witnessed an incredible turnabout in the making:

Almost overnight the nation has moved away from an official position of atheism and hostility to become perhaps the most open mission field in the world. Wherever we went, officials invited us to set up relief work, exchange programs, study centers, and religious publishing ventures. We heard reports that Young Life was inheriting camps from the Young Communists, and that the Gideons frantically were trying to resupply Bibles to hotel rooms (guests kept stealing them). Twenty-five hundred Soviet radio stations were carrying James Dobson's 'Focus on the Family' program—more than in the United States, Canada, and the rest of the world combined. Campus Crusade staff members were preparing a curriculum on Christianity for the public schools.[2]

Yancey is not the only one stunned; the whole world is agog over what God is doing in the largest nation on earth. Sometimes when we witness our Lord performing a turn-about such as this over a long period of time, we forget how impossible it seems. So to remind us just how astounding these recent changes are, I'd like to juxtapose some sayings of famous Marxists and Soviets with news of what's already taken place. I think you'll agree—some of God's turnabouts are like molasses in January: they take a long time, but my, are they sweet!

———◆———

"Religion is the sigh of the oppressed creature,
the sentiment of a heartless world,
and the soul of soulless conditions.
It is the opium of the people"

KARL MARX
Critique of Hegel's Philosophy of Right

Religion might be the opium of the people, but a deep, real, and growing relationship with Jesus Christ is their elixir of life...and they know it.

They instinctively recognize one of life's most unchanging truths as expressed by Augustine of Hippo, the great fourth-century Christian theologian:

> You made us for Yourself,
>   and our heart is restless,
>   until it rests in You.

Billy Graham highlighted this truth when he came to Moscow in late 1992 for an extraordinary three days of public ministry. He later said, "I've never seen such hunger for spiritual things. We believe that this is only the beginning of a movement of God in all the republics."[3]

A crusade counselor from the Ukraine agreed with him: "Many of these people want to believe, and maybe do believe, but nearly 75 years of communism have so affected them that they cannot grasp that they have the freedom to choose to come to Christ. I feel God is behind all the political reform."[4]

"We must fight against religion.
This is the ABC of all materialism,
and consequently, of Marxism."

VLADIMIR LENIN
1909

Major General David Robinson of the U.S. Army was in the Soviet Union in June 1991, conducting staff talks with the Soviet General Staff. He realized how much things were beginning to change when he asked to visit Lenin's tomb in Red Square. He wanted to hear the funereal music, see the red marble, the strict guards, and Lenin's body preserved in a glass-enclosed casket. General Robinson continues:

> When we got there, my host quietly requested that I not go inside. "You see, sir," he said, "the time has come to bury Lenin and be done with it!" His words hit me like an electric shock. They wanted to bury the father of communism and be done with it!...

> "You know," said my counterpart, "many people are turning to spiritual matters in our country. Things here are very difficult." I asked my friends why this was happening, but they did not know.[5]

In an attempt to keep the conversation going, General Robinson mentioned John's dramatic account of the third angel in the eighth chapter of Revelation who announced a devastating judgment on the rivers and springs of earth. John says a "star" called "Wormwood" poisoned the water (or made it "bitter") and killed many people. The general was surprised at his hosts' reaction.

99

> These words shocked my Russian escorts. I asked, through our interpreter, how the word "Wormwood," which means "Bitterness," is translated into Russian. The translation is *Chernobyl!* My hosts had a look of disbelief. They told me that the waters had turned bitter in the vicinity of the Chernobyl reactor, that many people had died and that others had suffered in the devastation of the meltdown. These words in the Book of Revelation attracted their attention beyond idle curiosity. How could such things have been written so long ago?[6]

How, indeed? Ah, what surprises God has in store for those who look for His turnabouts!

─────◆─────

"In this communal room, no one is ever bored,
For in the most visible place
hangs the portrait of Lenin.
To you, happy children, he opens the whole world,
He looks at us with a big smile, as if about to speak.
Be happy, little ones,
Grandchildren of the October Revolution."

SOVIET NURSERY SCHOOL SONG

Few people are more miserable than those who are ordered to be happy. A joke common among the Russian people before the final breakup of the Soviet Union went like this: "Adam and Eve were Russian, you know. It's a logical deduction. They were improperly clothed, possessed only one apple among them, and someone was always telling them they lived in paradise!"[7]

But the heart knows better. One can wear a smile even while drowning in despair. The 1992 Billy Graham crusade in Moscow served to point up the fact. When asked about the crusade, one Russian church leader commented, "We are living in a new era. For the last 70 years we have lived under a totalitarian regime where we were given recipes for complete and absolute happiness. Now instead of quoting Marx and Lenin, we are able to quote the Bible. Instead of Party meetings, we are able to hold religious services."[8]

Some Russian soldiers might have made this point the best. One night at the crusade the Russian Army Chorus sang, accompanied by its orchestra. After singing two pieces in Russian, members sang the "Battle Hymn of the Republic" in English. When they came to the words, "Glory! Glory! Hallelujah! His truth is marching on!" the entire stadium crowd spontaneously rose to its feet. When

100

the invitation was given to accept Christ, military personnel from the Army, Navy, Air Force, and Border Guards came forward to fill out an inquirer's card. A colonel later told Graham, "We are seeing spiritual renewal in the military. Even the military chorus, who once sang songs about Lenin, now sing spiritual songs."[9]

*"The Party cannot be neutral toward religion
and it does conduct anti-religious propaganda
against all and every religious prejudice...
Antireligious propaganda is the means by which
the complete liquidation of the reactionary clergy
must be brought about."*

JOSEPH STALIN
1927

The Graham crusade was held October 23 through 25 in Olympic Stadium, a facility built for the 1980 Olympic games. It was promoted through a massive ad campaign, the largest in Russian history. Advertisements appeared on radio, TV, and the sides of buses; they were placed in newspapers and even were hung on banners across busy streets. All of them brandished one question: "Why?" The ads went for the jugular to ask the central question about the meaning of life. Moscow homes were deluged with 3.2 million flyers, all calling their attention to "Vozrozhdeniye [Renewal] '92 with Billy Graham."[10]

Peter Deyneka, president of Russian-American Spiritual Renewal, could hardly believe what he was seeing.

Until a year ago last September, this Mission was not possible. The Party limited Christian activity. The Church did what it could, but it was limited. This was by far the largest organized evangelistic

101

movement ever, and it has affected the entire nation. It has attracted people from across the Commonwealth of Independent States. This effort has done more than anything else in the history of the Russian Church to unite the Church. This Mission has brought churches together, and for the first time in history they have come together cross-confessionally.

In the follow-up centers we are thrilled at what is going to happen. The structure is here for new converts. It's the book of Acts."[11]

───────◆───────

"If you meet with difficulties in your work,
or suddenly doubt your abilities,
think of him—of Stalin—and you will find
the confidence you need.
If you feel tired in an hour when you should not,
think of him—of Stalin—and your work will go well.
If you are seeking a correct decision, think of him—
of Stalin—and you will find that decision."

Pravda
February 17, 1950

102

Billy Graham visited Moscow in 1959 and prayed that one day the gospel could be proclaimed there in a public arena. He could not have known that the time would come when his arrival would be greeted with far more genuine gratitude than Stalin ever generated.

"Billy Graham is a historical person with historical significance," said Victor Hamm, a Russian evangelist who served as Graham's interpreter. "He has come to a country that is at a crossroads—that is not by chance. The prayers of many people have been answered."[12]

Basil, a rough-hewn Russian who preached for years to fellow prisoners in a Soviet labor camp, had no thoughts of Stalin when, one year before the crusade, he greeted Yancey's group during its 1991 visit. He did, however, think of Graham: "We have been through the valley of tears. When Billy Graham came in 1959 they let him appear on a balcony but not speak. To think that you are here in Moscow, the center of unbelief, able to talk and drink tea with the leaders of our country. It's a miracle! Brothers and sisters, be bold! With your wings you are lifting up children of the Lord. Where I come from the believers are praying for you at this minute. We believe your visit will help reach our country for God. May God bless you all."[13]

---

*"The number of people who believe in God
is growing less and less;
the youth are growing up, and the overwhelming
majority do not believe in God.
The enlightenment of the people,
the spread of scientific knowledge,
the study of the laws of nature
leaves no room for belief in God."*

NIKITA KHRUSHCHEV
1957

103

Khrushchev, it turns out, erred on a number of fronts. By fall 1992, radio evangelist Earl Poysti received an average of 120 responses a day from his Russian listeners—even before he was given access to the two thousand-station national network. The Christian Broadcasting Network also reported that 5 million viewers responded to their prime-time gospel programs during 1992.[14]

And then there's the October crusade—or shall we call it the October revolution? The first evening of the event,

Olympic Stadium quickly filled with a record crowd. People pushed through the doors at 4:30 P.M. for a 7:00 P.M. meeting. At night's end, the announcer pleaded with the people, "Don't leave all together. The Metro cannot accept all of you at once."[15]

By Sunday, 50,000 eager listeners jammed a stadium designed for a maximum of 38,000. Another 20,000 to 30,000 shivered in an outdoor plaza area equipped with a TV screen twenty feet high by thirty feet wide.

The first night of the crusade, 10,641 inquiry cards were turned in. The next night, the number rose to 12,628. And on the final day, the count skyrocketed to 19,417.

One important part of any Billy Graham crusade is the school of evangelism, where lay people can learn how to share their faith effectively. The Youth School of Evangelism attracted almost five thousand young people between the ages of sixteen and twenty-five from all areas of the former Soviet Union. A special children's mission called "Hide 'n' Seek" was held at the Palace of Creativity, a site formerly used to train Young Pioneers (a Communist youth organization). With the permission of the Russian Minister of Education, children were bused from schools twice a day for five days—almost ten thousand kids—to see and hear gospel presentations using drama, puppets, and singing designed to communicate the biblical parables of the lost coin, the lost sheep, and the prodigal son.

People got to the crusade however they could. A total of 360 buses were chartered for the meetings—more than for the Olympics twelve years earlier. And speaking of twelve, twelve chartered trains brought people from outside Moscow to the crusade. In Murmansk, near the Arctic Circle, one church hired three carriages on a train so Christians could bring along 150 unbelievers. The sponsoring pastor said that he and his parishioners live where once many Christians were imprisoned and died for their faith. "This is our time," he said. "We are in a hurry, and we cannot wait!"[16]

"We should remember Lenin's words,
that in our society everything which serves
to build up communism is moral."

LEONID BREZHNEV

Despite seventy-five years of effort, Soviet communism never succeeded in building a moral foundation for its people. The invitation sent by the chairman of the Supreme Soviet to Philip Yancey admits this. "In the difficult, often agonizing transitional period that our country is experiencing," it said, "spiritual and moral values acquire a great, if not paramount significance in their ability to guarantee us against confrontation, civil conflicts, the erosion of moral foundations, and the lowering of standards...."[17]

Other members of the Russian establishment have not been so vague in their critiques. Lieutenant Colonel Anatoly Belov of the Russian Army said one of the reasons he became a Christian was his observation of Christians in the military: "Working in the Military Tribunal, I noticed that soldiers who are believers carry out their military duty in a more responsible way. They are better disciplined, more honest and don't drink. Often their only request is to be permitted to go to a church or worship house on Sunday."[18]

Even non-Christians have noticed the moral difference between those who believe and those who don't. Lieutenant Colonel Mikhail Smyslov of the Russian Army says there are many things about evangelical Christians that commend his respect, including a

> meticulous compliance with the main moral postu-
> lates...of the Moral Code of the Constructor of

105

Communism! This very Code, adopted by the XII
Congress of the CPSU, was remembered by a number of our former leaders only in their public
speeches from high podiums, while in private they
wallowed in corruption and bribery. Baptists consider the principles set forth in this Code to be
important—principles such as honesty, truthfulness,
moral purity and mutual respect. After all, these
principles were first set forth by God in the Bible.[19]

Smyslov is not completely sold on Christians in the military, but he admits recent events have given him pause:

When our society began to turn to God again, amazing things started happening. Talking recently to
Major A. Ermakov, who not long ago was a political officer, I heard that he appointed as club manager in his military construction detachment a Baptist,
Sergeant V. Gamayunov. I asked Ermakov, "Did
you know that he was Baptist?"

"Sure, I knew. But I also know that the club will be
in ideal order, nothing will be stolen and all planned
events will be run on time. And, in general, I can
fully rely on all ten Baptists serving in our detachment."[20]

*"The struggle against religion is not a campaign,
not an isolated phenomenon,
not a self-contained entity;
it is an inseparable component...an essential link
and necessary element in the complex
of Communist education."*

PRAVDA
January 12, 1967

Smyslov is one of a number of Russians who have yet to embrace Christ, but who still stand amazed at the changes which rock their country. He writes:

> Our society has realized that progress toward the bright future of Communism has come to a deadlock. The society itself is on the verge of crisis. The attitude toward religion, and in particular toward Orthodoxy, that is tightly linked with the roots of Russian culture, has changed drastically. New church inaugurations have followed one another. Clergy have come out of hiding. Greeted with a roar of applause, they have taken honorary positions in many public agencies, including government. Evangelical Baptists have also straightened their shoulders. Now, very few people hide their beliefs when drafted. What would be the point of hiding it?
>
> "Nine Baptists are serving in our military construction detachment," I was told by the deputy of a military construction detachment, Captain S. Bogatyrev.
>
> "Do you carry out any atheistic propaganda among them?" I asked.
>
> "No. We are quite satisfied with their religion. No drinking, no smoking, no AWOLs. They don't violate the uniform regulations, and at work each of them is worth three men. In addition, they ask for nothing but for a leave to go to their worship house on Sunday."
>
> "Do you let them go?"
>
> "Sure, we know they will not let us down and will be back right on time. They are excellent servicemen, and the officers highly respect them."[21]

When God is in the midst of a great turnabout—especially one in the making for three-quarters of a century—everybody takes notice...even when they don't want to.

———◆———

"[I am calling for] a decisive and uncompromising struggle against manifestations of religion and strengthening of political work
with the masses and of atheist propaganda."

MIKHAIL GORBACHEV
1986

"I must say that for a long time I have drawn comfort from the Bible.
Ignoring religious experience has meant great losses for society.
And, I must acknowledge that Christians are doing much better than our political leaders
on the important questions facing us."

108

MIKHAIL GORBACHEV
1991

They say that foxholes make believers out of everybody, but the same might also be said of rapid political shifts. As the former Soviet Union began to disintegrate, Mikhail Gorbachev began to change his tune. In some ways, he had little choice. One joke common in Moscow in those days highlighted his difficulties: "The present government plan offers two ways to rebuild the country and reform society—a fantasy way and a realistic way. The first way is for everyone to work hard, joining together to become fully committed to *perestroika*, so that each one may contribute to social reconstruction. That is the *fantasy* way. Then there is the *realistic* way: The society will be saved by Martians."[22]

Muscovites got even more pointed than that, however. Writer Tomas C. Oden said that the people laughed when he described the "Gorby" phenomenon in the West, and they joked that the difference between Gorbachev in Moscow and Washington is that in Washington he could be elected.[23]

But jokes could not make the central question go away. Just how could Russia's tottering society be saved?

———◈———

"What good is a street that doesn't lead to a church?"

FINAL LINE IN THE RUSSIAN FILM
Repentance

Lieutenant Colonel Anatoly Pschelintsev of the Russian Army, also serves as Chairman of the Russian Association of Military Christians. He recognizes the devastation wreaked upon his country by the government's contempt for God, but also senses a fresh wind blowing.

> After long years of silence and spiritual oppression, people finally may breath freely. The moral decay of our society went to an extreme. Seventy years of wandering in the morally barren deserts of the secular state took its toll. Our people showed qualities uncharacteristic for our national character—such as callousness, cruelty, moral slackness and lack of spiritual values. Wonderful qualities like charity, self-negating love and compassion were wrung out of our hearts. People realize this loss and lean toward God.[24]

109

Then Pschelintsev makes a comment that screams off the page: "At this time there is no need to invent a new ideology to replace communism. One was developed long ago —Christianity."

That, my friends, is a turnabout of incomprehensible dimensions. As Pogo might say, "Who woulda thunk it?" Certainly, not many did. Not even many Christians. Not even Christians who believe God performs His turnabouts in the unlikeliest of circumstances and in the most unusual time frames. That is to say, not I. It never entered my head.

But then, it didn't really have to. God is not bound by my puny ability to comprehend His power and His plan. Nevertheless, it is good, after the fact, to look back and wonder at what He has done. To dream of what He might do—in the world or in your life.

Standing in awe of this mind-numbing turnabout, it only seems appropriate to let *Izvestiia*, the atheist voice of the former Soviet Union pronounce the benediction: *"Truly the ways of the Lord are inscrutable."*[25]

Amen, *Izvestiia*. Amen.

Chapter 7

Banana Peels Under the Oppressor's Boot

Most of us have seen at least portions of Leni Riefenstahl's classic 1935 film, *Triumph of the Will.* You might not remember the title, but its images are unforgettable.

The movie chronicles the Nuremberg Rally of 1934, a propaganda event carefully staged to display the glories of National Socialism in pre-war Germany. However shriveled their souls, the Nazis knew how to put on a good show.

Riefenstahl skillfully captured the "blaring Wagnerian overtures, stirring martial songs, banners, goose-step marches, human swastika formations, torchlight processions, bonfires, and magnificent fireworks displays. Adolf Hitler and other Nazi leaders delivered lengthy orations. Buildings were festooned with enormous flags and Nazi insignia."[1]

The film stirs powerful emotions even today, despite our full knowledge of later Nazi atrocities. I've seen parts of the movie many times, and I think the most stirring scenes are panoramic shots of goose-stepping soldiers marching past hundreds of thousands of exuberant party supporters. There is a fierce elegance in the clockwork stride of stern-faced, uniformed soldiers marching in deadly precision.

I have to admit, however, the spectacular scene also triggers a renegade thought: wouldn't it have been funny if thousands of banana peels had been thrown under the soldiers' feet and simultaneously upended the whole army? What a hilarious and ignominious heap of posteriors that would have revealed! Nazism might have died right there, as it deserved to. But alas, Mel Brooks was born too late.

Such an imagined scene unavoidably reminds me of Psalm 73:18-20:

> Surely you place them [the wicked]
>> on slippery ground;
>> you cast them down to ruin.
> How suddenly are they destroyed,
>> completely swept away by terrors!
> As a dream when one awakes,
>> so when you arise, O LORD,
>> you will despise them as fantasies.

Don't think this is mere Jewish rhetoric; the words remain as true today as when they were penned thousands of years ago. The might and prosperity of the wicked can still vanish in an instant. And sometimes, God unsheathes a turnabout that transforms their very conspiracies into thoroughfares of blessing for the feet of the oppressed.

Not Even ACME Can Help

This is an equal opportunity paperback. Earlier I spotlighted Speedy Gonzales, a rapid rodent who thrashes his enemies at breakneck speed. To prove I am not prejudiced against any members of the cartoon animal kingdom, I think it's only fair that I also honor a member of the bird family: Road Runner.

Road Runner is enmeshed in one of the longest-standing wars in cartoon history. It's hard to see why, though; Wile E. Coyote has yet to win a single battle. Almost every incident ends with the viewer staring down an immense cliff, a tiny puff of smoke marking the point of impact where Wile E. kissed the canyon floor. But the coyote will not give up.

He enlists the help of a stunning variety of traps, gizmos, weapons, widgets, and other contraptions to capture (and supposedly eat) his avian prey. ACME is his favorite supplier, but not even that ingenious company can get him over the hump to victory. Just when it looks as if his plot cannot fail, it does. Spectacularly.

113

I was invited to a friend's home the other night for a party. The festivities included a rented video tape of Baby Boomer memorabilia, including a Road Runner cartoon. In one brief scene Wile E. is set to pull the trigger on a massive catapult loaded with a gargantuan boulder. He has worked out the stone's trajectory and is waiting for Road Runner to appear. When the bird rockets by, the coyote pulls the rope to fire the catapult…and the force of his tug topples the rock directly upon his aching head. He can't win for losing.

I believe God has developed His own form of Road Runner theology. He delights in transforming the evil of men into marvelous manifestations of His infinite power and wisdom. When He sets Himself to overturn the wicked designs of evil men, not even ACME can prevent it.

One Dictator's Nightmare

Some months after the fall of the brutal Romanian dictator Nicolae Ceausescu, a good friend of mine traveled through that country with an unusual group of Americans. The little company included nurses, physical therapists, social workers, parents of mentally handicapped children, and several severely disabled men. They were led by the celebrated quadriplegic author and artist Joni Eareckson Tada.

What made the visit of these Americans so ironic was that for thirty years, Ceausescu had told his people "We have no handicaps in Romania. Everyone in Romania has whole, healthy bodies." Which being translated, meant, if you had a disability of any sort at all, you were a non-person. You were hidden away in an attic or a basement or back room, never to appear in public or offend the sensibilities of the "whole-bodied" citizenry enjoying the fruits of Ceausescu's atheistic, worker's paradise.

If you had the misfortune of being *born* with a disability, the prospects were very grim. International relief workers entering the country after the bloody overthrow of the Communist regime were shocked and sickened to find black, unspeakably filthy mediaeval dungeons filled with babies and toddlers judged "imperfect" by government standards.

Into this chamber of horrors came a laughing, smiling, singing woman in a power wheel chair, flanked by forty of the most skilled, loving, caring individuals you could ever hope to load on a single airplane. Once on Romanian soil, the group split up to take their technical skills, boundless compassion, and message of hope in Jesus Christ to the major cities across the country. Slowly at first, almost shyly, and then with a joyous rush, the Romanian people responded to the outreach. Disabled men, women, and children and their families came out of the attics and basements to attend

114

seminars, church services, and city-wide evangelistic rallies.

In the northern city of Cluj, occurred an incident my friend will never forget. Joni's team was holding an evangelistic rally in one of the city's major indoor sports arenas. The building was filled to overflow capacity, with tens of thousands more watching via regional television coverage. During the traditional greetings, various civic leaders and selected children approached the platform with armloads of flowers for Joni, her husband Ken, and other members of the team. All of this seemed polite and proper and unremarkable until one little boy walked up to the platform all by himself.

The little boy had no arms, and the single flower he carried for Joni was tucked under his chin. A hush fell over the audience and—for just a moment—there seemed to be no one else in all the world but one pretty lady in a wheelchair and one small lad who had probably never been seen much in public, let alone on Romanian television.

Joni received the flower, and then smiling through her tears, she turned to the audience. 115

"My little friend and I are going to demonstrate something you may have never seen before. He doesn't have any arms, and my arms are paralyzed. But do you know what? If you have love in your heart, you don't need arms to hug!"

Joni called the boy to her side and—with heads together, chins over each other's shoulders—demonstrated Romania's first "neck hug." And in that country that had been so cruelly schooled to close its eyes to deformity and close its heart to the humanity of the disabled, two of God's choice children gave a lesson in the triumph of love.

Ceausescu would not have been pleased. God must have been *very* pleased. "It was," my friend told me, "like a fragile flower poking up through the ashes, for the whole nation to see."

No Night Too Dark

If the saints can look down from heaven on the affairs of men, I know of someone else who must have been pleased, too. Thousands of years ago Isaiah peered into the future and wrote of the coming Messiah, "a bruised reed he will not break, and a smoldering wick he will not snuff out" (Isaiah 42:3). Now, in Romania, the Messiah's gentle, mighty work was beginning through the "weakest" members of Romanian society.

Later in their Romanian odyssey, Joni and several team members gathered in an ornate conference room in the palatial Hall of Deputies in Bucharest. Their meeting place was mere yards away from the upstairs balcony where the dictator used to stand before the masses and praise the virtues of atheistic communism. The Americans met with nine Romanian senators, who soberly asked Joni to pray for them—right then—and for their newly liberated nation. In a strong yet tender voice, this severely disabled woman, who just a few months before would have been considered a "non-person," invoked the blessing of Jesus Christ over the bowed heads of the country's leaders.

That, friends, is what I call a *turnabout!*

What's Deeper than a Well?

I'm pretty sure I understand what Isaiah meant in the passage I just quoted, but not all Scripture is so immediately clear to me. Consider a little verse in the book of Hebrews, for example. It always struck me a little odd that the writer of Hebrews 11 chose to honor the Old Testament patriarch Joseph with these words:

> By faith Joseph, when his end was near, spoke about the exodus of the Israelites from Egypt and gave instructions about his bones (Hebrews 11:22).

About his bones? *Who cares?* Had I been assigned to edit his manuscript, I probably would have written a memo to the following effect:

Dear contributor:

Hi! I just wanted to take this opportunity to thank you for all the hard work you've put in on your part of the Bible project. The whole thing is shaping up nicely, and I think your contribution is one of its highlights. Congratulations!

I love the way you set the tone for the book from the outset. Your majestic portrait of the Son is breathtaking, and the way you compare and contrast the new covenant with the old is excellent. Great job!

I've already written to you about some problems that I think readers might have with parts of chapters 6 and 10. It'd be no good to make people scratch their heads and wonder just exactly what you mean! But I'm sure you'll take care of all of that. Thanks for your prompt attention to the matter.

117

I do have one more teensy suggestion to make in the manuscript. It looks great overall, but...what were you thinking in 11:22? The life of Joseph takes up almost a full thirty percent of the book of Genesis—fourteen out of fifty chapters—and you highlight his funeral arrangements? I'd really like you to rethink this. Genesis reports many powerful incidents in Joseph's life that would better illustrate his deep faith. Why'd you pick bones, anyway? Look, if the deadline is too stressful for you, we could move it back a few weeks. I'd rather do that and have a bestseller on our hands than push to meet the schedule and wind up with...well, bones.

Do you see what I mean? I'm anxious to speak with you about this. Call me when you get the chance.

Meanwhile, thanks for a *super* effort. With a little more work, this manuscript could really go places!

Sincerely in Him,

Stephanos

It's a good thing I wasn't in the publishing business two thousand years ago. The way it stands, Hebrews 11:22 demonstrates an ingenious aspect of Scripture. Some things in the Bible are deliberately unclear for the simple reason that God wants us to sweat a little before we come up with the answer. It's a technique that separates the men from the boys, the genuinely interested from the merely curious. Jesus did it all the time with His parables. Those who really want to know what God means in a perplexing text will dig until they hit pay dirt; those who think of the Bible as a religious Trivial Pursuit game will pass and move on to more "exciting" categories.

I now think the mention of Joseph's burial details is a shorthand way of calling to mind the patriarch's sterling character as well as his amazing prophetic career. God doesn't hand out prophecies of the central event of the Old Testament—the exodus—to just anybody. This reference in Hebrews is intended to remind us just what an immense figure Joseph was and that he remained faithful to God until his dying day.

Had the writer of Hebrews chosen to dwell on a more extended incident from Joseph's life, however, he may well have decided to highlight a text from Genesis 50. A verse in that chapter has done as much to comfort God's people during episodes of human ruthlessness as perhaps any other biblical passage.

But before I reproduce it, I should briefly rehearse where Joseph had been before the Holy Spirit prompted him to utter the soothing words.

Joseph was his father's pet. Jacob never even tried to hide his favoritism from his other sons; in fact, he flaunted it by lavishing on Joseph special gifts and treatment. That was why Joseph's brothers hated him and decided to make him disappear.

One day they saw Joseph approaching in the distance and a hateful plan began to coalesce in their minds. They attacked him, stripped him, and threw him down a well while they debated his fate. Trapped in a deep hole, Joseph had to wonder how much further his fortunes could sink. *Not much deeper*, he may have thought. Wrong.

His brothers sold him as a slave to a group of roving Midianite merchants, and for the next several years, whenever things began to look up for Joseph, his world came crashing down. He lurched from a position of favor to a jail cell, from a chance at freedom to continued imprisonment. God seemed to be nowhere…

Until it was God's time.

In a swift turn of events utterly characteristic of the way God often operates, Joseph became the second most powerful man in Egypt. Eventually the brothers who betrayed him were placed in his hands. He could do to them what he willed. Kill them? Torture them? Enslave them? Let them go free? The brothers were terrified. Who wouldn't be? But this is what Joseph told them:

> You intended to harm me, but God intended it for good to accomplish what is now being done, the saving of many lives (Genesis 50:20).

119

Joseph was God's man and he wanted above all to please his heavenly Master. He knew that God ruled, not the evil choices of wicked men. And Joseph knew God was a God of turnabouts.

God was in complete control of the whole seeming mess. He took undeniably evil acts and turned them inside out to His everlasting glory...but also allowed one of His choice servants to remain in the dark (figuratively and literally) for a very long time.

This is not at all atypical of the way God does things. He might be at work in your life in just this fashion right now. You could be locked in some prison this moment—whether of walls and bars or of emotional chains, it makes little difference—and are wondering why God does not seem interested in rescuing you. You might even be wondering, *can God do it? Is He able to rescue me from my enemy's hands?*

Joseph's story teaches us that God still sits on the throne of the universe. It is an effortless thing for the Lord to reverse human evil. It is not at all challenging. We should not imagine Him straining to figure out how He might use the actions of wicked men and women to further His holy purposes. One of my favorite authors, John Piper, puts it like this:

> People lift their hand to rebel against the Most High only to find that their rebellion is unwitting service in the wonderful designs of God. Even sin cannot frustrate the purposes of the Almighty.

> Similarly, when we come to the end of the New Testament and to the end of history in the Revelation of John, we find God in complete control of all the evil kings who wage war. In Revelation 17, John speaks of a harlot sitting on a beast with ten horns.

The harlot is Rome, drunk with the blood of the saints; the beast is the antichrist and the ten horns are ten kings "who give over their power and authority to the beast...[and] make war on the Lamb."

But are these evil kings outside God's control? Are they frustrating God's designs? Far from it. They are unwittingly doing his bidding. "For God has put it in their hearts to carry out his purpose by being of one mind and giving their royal power to the beast, until the words of God shall be fulfilled" (Revelation 17:17). No one on earth can escape the sovereign control of God: "The king's heart is a stream of water in the hand of the Lord; he turns it wherever he will" (Proverbs 21:1; cf. Ezra 6:22).[2]

At the beginning of his trials, Joseph probably wondered if he could descend any deeper than the well into which his brothers had tossed him. Then he found out the answer—yes, it could get deeper. Much deeper. First there was slavery. Then exile into Egypt. Then false accusations. Then 121 prison for at least two years. When he finally reached the bottom of the pit, to his amazement he discovered something deeper still. Curiously, however, he had to look up to see it.

They say that when you're in the bottom of a very deep well, you can see stars. If that's true, then Joseph saw myriad galaxies all blazing with unquenchable light. Perhaps that's what helped him keep going in those long years when everything he did seemed to turn out wrong. Deep in the pit he looked up, saw God's stars, and knew that the same limitless power that placed those stars in the heavens could also lift him to high places. The deepest thing of all in Joseph's life was the wisdom and love of God.

The same is true for you. Turnabout is God's play—even with the evil deeds of wicked men and women. God can and does take human evil and turn it inside out for His glory. What a dazzling God we serve!

Operation Desert Turnabout

God is at work reversing human evil all over the globe. One noteworthy example is found in the Middle East.

Saddam Hussein's 1990 invasion of Kuwait actually paved the way for evangelistic success in his own country. Until recently, the Kurdish peoples were isolated from the rest of the world behind formidable barriers—geographic, political, and cultural. Kurdistan stretches from eastern Turkey, across northern Iraq and into northwestern Iran. The Kurds number about 25 million and had been largely untouched by the gospel.

Until Saddam.

"Before the Gulf War," said one report, "Iraqi Kurdistan had become a slaughterhouse. Saddam's troops waged a vicious genocidal campaign in the restricted area, and the Iraqi dictator instructed his armies to 'leave neither man nor beast alive.'"[3] Somehow, the international community virtually ignored the carnage. But God didn't.

Operation Desert Storm crippled Saddam's military capabilities and led to the establishment of a security zone in northern Iraq the following year. Following its victory, the U.S. military launched Operation Provide Comfort, one of the largest relief efforts in history.

As food and clothing flooded into the devastated country, concerned Christians in 1992 alone built more than four thousand houses for Kurdish war victims. One U.S. military insider reported that Christian organizations are responsible for more than 90 percent of all relief operations in Iraqi Kurdistan.

What sort of response are these Christians provoking? "They have been invited to share their faith everywhere," said one source, "and Christian literature is in great demand. One Arabic-speaking evangelist said he recently distributed 172 gospel portions on a street corner in less than forty minutes, and he added that border agents have asked for their own copies."[4]

Dudley Woodberry of Fuller Seminary's School of World Mission has reported that nearly the entire Kurdish town of As-Sulaymaniyah in eastern Iraq has begun to consider Christianity. He says Kurds there are "rejecting Islam because they don't want a religion capable of producing a tyrant like Saddam Hussein."[5]

Even in Saudi Arabia, the home of Mecca and the heart of the Islamic world, marked changes have followed in the wake of the Gulf War. The Bible is now more available there than in any time in history—but it took an angry General Norman Schwarzkopf to make it happen. When the U.S. military first asked for Bibles to be allowed into the country to meet the needs of American troops, the request was summarily denied. Schwarzkopf quickly let his considerable displeasure be known, however, and Arabic-and English-language Bibles began flooding into the country. Even today, God's Word is being airlifted in on cargo flights where space is available. Perhaps most remarkably, it's not unusual to see Third World nationals carrying the distinctive "Desert Storm camouflage" New Testaments on Saudi streets.[6]

God is at work in the spiritual center of the Muslim world, employing human evil to pave the way for divine blessing. Of course, human wickedness isn't confined to the Middle East in the person of Saddam Hussein. There's plenty of it to go around.

123

Phosphorous Grenades and the Gospel

Franklin Graham, head of Samaritan's Purse, a Christian relief agency, tells of an unforgettable encounter he had a few years ago in Lebanon. Human evil there led directly to the salvation of an entire Lebanese family.

The Hajj family lived in the village of Aintura, rebuilt after a 1977 shelling. The town was strategically located above a Syrian military encampment armed with artillery.

One day the Syrians claimed a shot from Aintura had been fired at their camp, so they began to brutally depopulate the village. They ranged through the town hurling grenades into shops and houses, incinerating the whole town. When soldiers found the Hajj family huddled in their kitchen, they tossed a phosphorous grenade into the room and held the door shut to prevent anyone from escaping.

All three children, the husband and the mother were horribly burned. A grandmother perished in the assault. The mother, Isobelle, was so badly scorched that scar tissue on her arms and hands and chest had fused. Her arms were useless.

124

And yet, this attack was the very means God used to bring the entire family to faith. The Lord did not prevent evil men from inflicting monstrous pain—but He used that evil for His own glory. It happened like this.

Prior to the attack, the family had begun to study the Bible. But when the Syrians arrived, the husband thought it wisest to discontinue their investigations, since he was afraid what the newcomers might do if they learned of the study. Isobelle was saddened—she was beginning to understand and believe in Christ—but she obeyed the wishes of her husband. The attack convinced the family both of the depravity of man and of the hope of the gospel, and all placed their faith in Christ.

Still, there was the tragedy of Isobelle's useless arms. What could be done? Graham eventually persuaded one of the top plastic surgeons in the country to take up Isobelle's case, and over the course of a full year the mobility of her arms had been restored. Isobelle was overjoyed and wrote a letter to Graham:

> I took this pen with a trembling hand, not trembling from fear—but from joy and happiness, which is the first letter since my operation, which by the mercy of the Lord and your kindness has helped to restore.... Truly I had to suffer a lot during this year, but deep inside me I have had joy and comfort. And when I was alone, I always used to repeat in my heart why God has permitted this to happen. It was the door for our salvation and eternal life.[7]

Score another direct hit for divine turnabouts!

Afghanistan is another hot spot where fearsome shelling is opening doors to the gospel. By late 1992, Islamic fundamentalists had killed nearly three thousand people through vicious attacks on Kabul, capital of Afghanistan. Electricity, phones, television, and public transportation all were disrupted. During a lull in the fighting, a Christian missionary offered a ride to two elderly women. As they drove through a heavily-damaged section of the city, the two ladies cursed Islam and said if their religion was responsible for this destruction, they "wanted no part of it." After years of hardness, these ladies and others like them are responding to the gospel message. In fact, a high-ranking Muslim cleric who also serves as a close advisor to defense minister Ahmed Shah Masoud did something previously unheard of. The moment he was given a New Testament, the mullah read it to government officials seated around him. And may I relate one last evidence that God is turning human evil inside out

125

in Afghanistan? One fellowship in Kabul led 207 families to Christ during the winter of 1992.[8]

A similar story is being played out in the former "killing fields" of Cambodia. "The horror of Pol Pot's massacres and continuing economic hardships have produced what one denominational leader calls 'an unprecedented openness,' " says one report. "The Assemblies of God has reported three new churches as a by-product of humanitarian efforts, with another four in development...[and] in Kompong Chang, a city located about 100 miles northwest of Phnom Penh, a facility that formerly housed communist guerrillas was given to the Assemblies for use as a church building."[9]

Make no mistake, human evil is a monstrous thing. Its twentieth-century incarnation can rip and tear and crush and smother and intimidate at levels unimaginable in simpler eras. It is capable of the most barbarous acts and the most heinous crimes...but it is not able to prevent God from using its very evil for His own glory.

Turnabout is God's play! And human evil can never extend beyond His reach.

Darkness to Light

I have tried to make my point in this chapter by highlighting God's ongoing turnabouts all over the globe. But I fear my technique may tempt some to think that banana peels slide under the oppressor's boot primarily in foreign lands. Not so! God keeps an ample stock of the slippery skins in every nation of the world, including this one.

Karen Mains reminded me of this on a recent visit to the Chapel of the Air radio ministry. I had arrived in Wheaton, Illinois, the day Karen was to record a Christmas message for broadcast on December 25. I was privileged to help her tell a true story that also serves as a parable about divine turnabouts.

For many years the city of St. Charles, Illinois, lit up a star of Bethlehem to celebrate the Christmas season. But one day the courts decided the display served to "promote religion" and ordered it discontinued. The town obliged and the night sky went black.

But the following year, something strange happened. Two or three large, illuminated stars popped up over businesses and homes where once there had been nothing but air. The next year, several more stars lit up the heavens and a clear trend was growing. By Christmas 1992, hundreds of stars blazed from roofs and windows all over the city, wordlessly proclaiming Jesus' victory of light over darkness and righteousness over evil.

Now, I don't mean to suggest the courts were evil in what I believe to be a mistaken interpretation of the constitution; but I do mean that they have no jurisdiction over the residents of heaven. Especially the Landlord.

The glowing stars of St. Charles will forever remind me of Who reigns over the affairs of men and women. Turnabout is God's play! And no night is so dark that a Bethlehem star can't burn a hole clear through it.

127

Christmas, stars, and divine turnabouts. They all go together so nicely! But the more I think about it, the more I believe another symbol could be effectively added to this impressive list.

And no, I'm not thinking of a fir tree or poinsettia. While both certainly remind me of Christmas, their connection to divine turnabouts is a little less clear. No, when I think of Yuletide turnabouts these days, only one plant slips into my head, and it's neither a tree nor a potted plant.

It's the banana. Yippee!

Chapter 8

Mother Nature Does Handstands

*E*arly on the morning of July 28, 1976, most residents of the coal-mining and industrial city of T'ang-shan, China, were asleep. In a few hours, their normal routines called for them to rise from their beds, leave their unreinforced masonry homes, and go to work.

More than 240,000 of them never did.

That's the appalling estimate of deaths caused by a massive earthquake which nearly razed the city that morning. An additional 500,000 persons were injured in one of the worst natural disasters ever recorded.[1]

Did you know that about fifty thousand earthquakes large enough to be felt without instruments shake the earth each year? Approximately one hundred of them are big enough to cause major damage if they are centered near heavily populated areas. A quake in Lisbon, Portugal, on November 1, 1755, killed sixty thousand people in the capital alone. Another in the Tokyo-Yokohama metropolitan area on September 1, 1923, claimed the lives of more than 140,000 victims. And a huge earthquake in Alaska on March 27, 1964, killed only 131 persons, but dramatically reshaped the landscape: more than seventy-two thousand square miles were tilted, at one end sinking almost eight feet and at the other rising as high as eighty feet.[2]

It's this kind of overwhelming destructive power that we associate with earthquakes. We can't predict them and we certainly can't control them.

But God can.

In fact, He occasionally even *uses* earthquakes and other natural disasters in His service.

When Earth Shakes, Heaven Doesn't

Earthquakes. Hurricanes. Volcanoes. Floods. Plagues. Droughts. Fires. Illness. In devastating ways, the normal course of nature periodically flips out, shattering the comforting rhythms of day-to-day living. Wild forces beyond our control or understanding pulverize our plans and wreak havoc on our world. People are injured. Others lose everything they own. Still others die.

"Why?" we cry out. "Doesn't God care? Or is He too weak to do anything about it?"

Thousands of years ago, the prophet Jeremiah had some of the same questions. And although the answers he received were not exhaustive, they were enough. Jeremiah basically learned two things. First, he discovered that natural calamities are not outside the sovereign control of God:

> Who can speak and have it happen
> if the Lord has not decreed it?

130

Is it not from the mouth of the Most High
    that both calamities and good things come?
        (Lamentations 3:37-38).

But second, Jeremiah learned that God has a loving purpose even behind the wrenching disasters that threaten to swallow us whole:

For men are not cast off
    by the Lord forever.
Though he brings grief, he will show compassion,
    so great is his unfailing love.
For he does not willingly bring affliction
    or grief to the children of men
        (Lamentations 3:31-33).

In this chapter, I want to highlight God's love and mercy even in the midst of natural disasters and terrible illness. I want to recount His faithfulness even in the most trying of times. And I want us to rejoice in the certainty that no night is too stormy or dark for God to bring forth healing light.

131

A Life-Giving Earthquake

In Heaven's skillful hands, the same devastating forces that spawned the deadly T'ang-shan earthquake can give life rather than take it. The Bible describes at least one such benevolent seismic event.

Silas and the apostle Paul were on a missionary trip to Philippi when they were arrested, stripped, severely flogged, and thrown into prison. The jailer locked them in the inner cell and fastened their feet in stocks. Why? Because the pair had destroyed a local fortune-teller's business when they freed his slave girl—his source of income— from demon possession.

I've never been arrested, stripped, beaten, and tossed into maximum security, but my hunch is it'd be no fun. Yet Paul and Silas decided to hold an impromptu concert about midnight and their voices rang through the whole prison. Then something happened:

> Suddenly there was such a violent earthquake that the foundations of the prison were shaken. At once all the prison doors flew open, and everybody's chains came loose (Acts 16:26).

When the jailer saw what had happened, he drew his sword to kill himself, for he thought his prisoners had escaped. By Roman law, if your prisoners escape, you don't. Just as he was about to do himself in, Paul shouted, "Don't harm yourself! We are all here!" (Acts 16:28). When the man saw it was so, he "rushed in and fell trembling before Paul and Silas. He then brought them out and asked, 'Sirs, what must I do to be saved?'"

132

> They replied, "Believe in the Lord Jesus, and you will be saved—you and your household." Then they spoke the word of the Lord to him and to all the others in his house. At that hour of the night the jailer took them and washed their wounds; then immediately he and all his family were baptized. The jailer brought them into his house and set a meal before them; he was filled with joy because he had come to believe in God—he and his whole family (Acts 16:31-34).

Have you been counting the number of turnabouts in this passage? I came up with at least four: God used the power of a "violent earthquake" to:

1. Get the attention of a pagan jailer who quickly came to faith in the Lord Jesus;

2. Bring the jailer's whole family to trust in God;

3. Impress upon the rest of the prisoners that the message of Paul and Silas was worth hearing;

4. Prompt the jailer to use his personal resources to medicate and feed his former prisoners.

Notice I didn't even count in my total the missionaries' original incarceration. But without that hardship, the earthquake would have amounted to just another planetary hiccup.

Many earthquakes kill; but when God chooses to book one for a guest appearance in a turnabout, it gives life—eternal life. And earthquakes aren't the only unusual stars that appear on the Lord's unpredictable program.

Even the Wind and the Rain Obey Him

I grew up in a wonderful, evangelism-minded church in Beloit, Wisconsin. People's Church emphasized world missions, and from our youngest days we were exposed to missionaries serving in all parts of the globe.

Gene Thomas, a missionary to Africa with United World Mission, spoke often at People's. He had more than his share of exciting testimonies from the field, but I remember one in particular. Gene and his co-workers had been working long and hard with a particular tribe, but still hadn't won the people's trust. This tribe had little in the way of material goods and the missionaries determined to help them improve their standard of living. They were in the middle of a crucial building project in the heart of the village when a potential disaster rumbled on the horizon. The skies suddenly grew black and threatening, the winds began to howl, and the village workmen shot each other frightened, knowing glances. Everybody could see that a huge storm was blowing in—and everyone knew it would likely destroy everything they had labored to build.

133

All along the missionaries had been telling the Africans about a God of unimaginable power who loved them so much He had sent His only Son to die on their behalf. But was this God strong enough to stop the storm? For the Africans, it was a crucial test.

So Gene Thomas prayed. He prayed *hard*. When he was finished, he and everyone else looked up to see what would happen.

And this is what they saw: the dark, menacing clouds swept closer and closer, directly toward the village's unfinished structure. It looked as if everything would be flattened. At the last moment, something strange happened. The storm didn't abate nor did it stop—but it *split in two*, completely skirting the village. The building was spared, and God used the very storm that had threatened to set back the missionaries' labors to rocket them to a new level. Now the villagers were ready to listen...and believe. The God of turnabouts had proven His power once again.

134 **Goodness and Severity**

No one's life was taken when the violent earthquake hit the Philippian jail. No one in the African village was injured by the powerful storm that swept its perimeters. Sadly, it often doesn't happen that way. Pain and suffering are a part of life on a sin-warped planet. But in the hands of an almighty God, even horrible disasters can be turned into a channel of great blessing.

Paul talks in Romans 11:22 about the "goodness and severity of God (NASB)," elaborating on a solemn theme highlighted by Jesus Himself. In Luke 13, Jesus is informed about a group of Galileans whom Pilate had killed even while they were worshiping in the temple. Apparently they wondered if these men were great sinners for receiving such murderous treatment. Jesus wasted no time in setting straight their theology, and I'm not sure most seminaries would approve of the way He handled this piece of pastoral counseling. Jesus replied,

> Do you think that these Galileans were worse sinners than all the other Galileans because they suffered this way? I tell you, no! But unless you repent, you too will all perish. Or those eighteen who died when the tower in Siloam fell on them—do you think they were more guilty than all the others living in Jerusalem? I tell you, no! But unless you repent, you too will all perish (vv. 2-5).

His words sound harsh. Severe. Hardly the soft picture of a gentle Jesus which sells so many books nowadays. Of course, Jesus often was warm and reassuring and gentle; but He could also be tough, sarcastic, and even severe.

But don't think for a moment that this severity grew out of an erratic disposition or a poor night's sleep. "Severe" doesn't mean "unloving." It simply means that real love will do whatever it takes to care for the object of that love.

135

Jesus' hard words in these verses reflect His deep concern for the eternal well-being of His audience. In our natural state we are terminally ill and about to die; but our fever is so high we imagine we are the picture of health. Jesus' words are intended to cool our brows enough so that we can grasp our mortal danger.

Notice especially the Lord's comments about the Siloam tower disaster. Eighteen people died in the catastrophe, but all Jesus does is call attention to the spiritual peril of His hearers. He is not unconcerned about the dead, but their eternal destiny is sealed; there may yet be hope for His audience. In other words, Jesus wanted to use the Siloam disaster for a spiritual turnabout. God takes no pleasure in the death of the wicked and therefore mentioned the tower (without being prompted!) to shake to consciousness His spiritually sleepy hearers.

God's purposes are always good, but they may seem severe to people accustomed to sin. Even disasters can become mighty turnabouts in the hand of God.

An Ill Wind Blows Some Good

Hurricane Hugo slammed into the southeastern coast of the United States in September of 1989, demolishing homes and snuffing out lives wherever it raged. One Christian relief agency, Samaritan's Purse, provided over ninety mobile homes for families who lost everything. The agency also worked with the Mennonites, the Salvation Army, and other groups to rebuild and repair the damaged homes of the poor.

Relief workers met some Christian farmers from Johns Island, near Charleston, South Carolina, who every year hired migrant workers to harvest their crops. Living situations for most of the migrants were primitive at best, slums at worst. The hurricane had leveled these camps and the farmers needed help in repairing them. Without rebuilt facilities, the farmers could not hire the migrant workers and their crops would spoil.

Samaritan's Purse first began sending in work teams from concerned churches, then asked if it could begin a gospel outreach among the migrants. The organization brought in two Spanish-speaking evangelists, who did one-on-one evangelism and held preaching services in the evening. Christian films in Spanish were also shown. "This has yielded a great spiritual harvest," the relief agency reported. "Many of the migrant laborers have come from Mexico, Central America and the Caribbean to find work.

136

Many have been abused and exploited. In the months ahead we want to continue to show them God's love and give them the Gospel of Jesus Christ."[3]

Such a large, productive, multi-national outreach effort to such a disparate group of Spanish-speaking people could have *never* happened apart from the terrible devastation of that killer hurricane. But don't thank Hugo. All praise belongs to the God of turnabouts, who can make even the fury of a storm sing a doxology.

The Billy Graham Evangelistic Association also designated $25,000 from its World Emergency Fund to supplement over $35,000 collected in a special offering for hurricane relief.[4] And then Graham himself decided to take a whirlwind tour of coastal South Carolina, including the towns of Garden City, Hemingway, Awendaw, Sullivan's Island, and downtown Charleston.

"In Garden City," reported a newspaper article covering the evangelist's visit, "Graham pointed to the good things that have come from Hugo—people forgetting divisions and helping each other. He predicted that people who know Christ will be better able to deal with the inevitable stress to come." The reporter also noted that Graham "sensed the same spirit of hope and good will here that he felt in Northern California where he toured earthquake-struck towns."[5]

Graham insisted that those who prepare spiritually would find comfort when disaster struck.

"It was really what we waited for," said Charleston Fire Chief Wilmot E. Guthke, "to hear a message of encouragement, keep the faith and that we will survive and will come back." Nancy Swan of Mount Pleasant agreed with Graham that although the storm broke many hearts, it also left behind something that brought joy. "We're going to be so much stronger," she said. "As he said it, it's time to trust Jesus."[6]

Like many biblical storms which yielded a spiritual harvest (*see* Exodus 9:22-26; Jonah 1:14-16; Luke 8:22-25; Acts 27:13-26), even the furious winds of a class-five hurricane were made to serve the good purposes of God. This was precisely the lesson Job learned long ago, from the mouth of the very One who turns gales into glory:

> Then the LORD answered Job out of the storm.
> He said...
> Who cuts a channel for the torrents of rain,
> and a path for the thunderstorm...
> Can you raise your voice to the clouds
> and cover yourself with a flood of water?
> Do you send the lightning bolts on their way?
> Do they report to you, "Here we are"?
> (Job 38:1,25,34-35).

Job knew that God alone fits this awesome description. When the Almighty speaks, even fearsome storms leap to do His bidding.

138

Can a Virus Preach?

Still, nobody likes to suffer. Whether we're part of a great turnabout or not, suffering *hurts*. It isn't on anyone's top-ten list of Things to Do. We don't like it when natural disasters cause us pain. Fortunately, most of us won't have to deal with them throughout our lives. They blow in and blow out.

Not so with disease and sickness.

Viral infections, bacterial invasions, and other pathogens have entrenched themselves in our world ever since the Fall. Like natural disasters, they come at us from nowhere, cause us great pain, and can sometimes prompt us to doubt God's love.

Now, I am deeply grateful that God is still in the healing business and that He sometimes miraculously cures a supposedly incurable disease. But He doesn't always do so and—surprising as it may seem—we ought to be grateful that He doesn't. I'm sure the people of Galatia would agree.

The powerful little book of Galatians heads up a train of Pauline letters hitched to the apostle's "major" epistles of Romans and First and Second Corinthians. Sometimes it's called "little Romans" because it explores the theme of justification by faith, not by works. Except for a mysterious disease, however, we likely would never have been blessed with its liberating wisdom.

That might sound strange, but Paul himself explains what I mean:

> As you know, it was because of an illness that I first preached the gospel to you. Even though my illness was a trial to you, you did not treat me with contempt or scorn. Instead, you welcomed me as if I were an angel of God, as if I were Christ Jesus himself (Galatians 4:13-14).

139

The logic seems inescapable to me: without the illness, Paul would not have preached to the Galatians; had Paul not preached to the Galatians, they would not have come under his care; had they not come under his care, he would not have written them a book; and had he not written them a book, we could not read Galatians today.

It doesn't matter what kind of illness Paul suffered. The point is that God used a repulsive physical condition—a "trial" to the Galatians which might well have produced "contempt" or "scorn"—and used it bring the gospel to those who hadn't heard it (and a portion of Scripture to the church which needs it).

Turnabout is God's play—and some of His tools are as microscopic as viruses and bacteria.

A Ray of Sunshine

Ray Holder is the father of one of my good friends as well as the chaplain at Tuality Hospital in Hillsboro, Oregon. A hospital chaplain sees more heartache and ecstasy, sorrow and exhilaration in one year than most of us witness in a lifetime. It's a constant roller coaster of emotions from stratospheric highs to mine shaft lows. But it's also a profession privileged to witness some remarkable divine turnabouts.

One Monday morning a patient on the fifth floor of the hospital asked Ray to stop by. The chaplain had only been in his room a few minutes when the patient blurted out, "How can I be a real Christian, chaplain?" Ray was both surprised and pleased as he led the man to a saving relationship with Christ. The patient then explained he had been praying all night for himself and the man in the next room, who "was in very bad shape."

"As I left that room one of our Christian nurses rejoiced with me over our friend's salvation and said, 'I want you to see two others,'" Ray writes.

> One of them was the man in the next room suffering from emphysema who was in serious condition and slowly dying. He was an ex-logger who swore every other word, even when unconscious. His Christian nephew was there. We talked. I then spoke with the ex-logger and he seemed to understand. I briefly explained God's plan of salvation and prayed as he listened. When I asked him if he was trusting the Lord as his Savior, he said, "No—go on." I said I'd keep praying for him, talked briefly with his nephew, and left the room as he fell back into cursing again.[7]

140

As Ray left the room he described his encounter with the nurse, who said she knew the man and would speak with him. The Christian nurse spoke clearly, lovingly, and tenderly to the dying logger, while Ray visited an elderly woman unsure of her eternal destiny. While Ray was at work in one room and the nurse in the other, God was laboring in both rooms simultaneously, using illness for His glory in a heaven-sent turnabout. Ray reports:

> Both of these individuals prayed that morning to confess their sin to God and to place their faith in Jesus Christ as their very own personal Savior and Lord! The elderly woman read a prayer in a little booklet that I had given her and signed her name and date and then wrote underneath her signature, "I love you, Lord!" The ex-logger died later that evening. The next week his wife also became a believer in Christ as her neighbors—a retired pastor and his wife—lovingly cared for her and helped her in her grief. There were tears of joy on the fifth floor that day and in heaven, rejoicing over the salvation of these precious and special individuals.[8]

141

Turnabouts utilizing illness aren't reserved for salvation experiences alone, however; God may also use them in the lives of His beloved children.

One dear Christian lady approached Ray about her own illness: "Chaplain, I've been a Christian for many years. God has been so good to me in so many ways. I'm thankful—but it seems like I've been sick for over forty years! My body is all out of balance now and they just can't seem to tell what is causing all these problems. I'm so discouraged—I just don't know what to do!"[9]

Ray spoke with the woman and prayed with her before leaving the room, but it wasn't until the drive home later that evening that Paul's explanation of praying three times for the "thorn" in his flesh to be removed came to mind. When he got home, he looked up those famous verses in 2 Corinthians 12:9 and 10, and also saw that week's issue of *Moody Monthly* lying on his kitchen table. The following words by Joni Eareckson Tada caught his attention immediately:

> People with disabilities are God's best visual aids to demonstrate who He really is. His power shows up best in weakness. And who, by the world's standards, is weaker than the mentally or physically disabled? As the world watches, these people persevere. They live, love, trust and obey him. Eventually, the world is forced to say, "How great their God must be to inspire this kind of loyalty."[10]

Later that evening Ray called the patient at the hospital and related these ideas to her. "The next day her attitude was much improved," Ray writes. "Recently she was discharged from the hospital and went home. She thanked me a number of times for calling her that night and sharing that concept of a Christian's approach to disabilities and sickness."[11]

This kind of turnabout isn't likely to make the evening news or even Sunday's sermon. But it's a turnabout nevertheless, bringing glory to God and hope to His downcast people. The biblical text which Ray used in his counseling of the woman is worth a closer look.

Thorns and Roses

Franklin L. Stanton had definite ideas about roses and thorns, and his opinion is probably in the majority:

> This world that we're a-livin' in
> is mighty hard to beat;
> You git a thorn with every rose,
> But *ain't* the roses *sweet!*[12]

Most of us consider the bloom delightful and the thorn unfortunate. I do! But in the topsy-turvy world of divine turnabouts, the thorn sometimes *is* the bloom. That's what Paul discovered through a divinely-ordained personal trial.

The Corinthians were a difficult bunch. Of all the churches Paul planted, this one gave him the most trouble. That's why we have two letters to the Corinthians in our New Testaments; the first memorandum didn't come close to straightening out the mess, and in the second Paul warns the church that he's on his way to take care of matters personally.

One sore point with this church was its apparent refusal to take Paul seriously. Many in the congregation simply dismissed the apostle's authority. So beginning with chapter 10 of 2 Corinthians, Paul begins to build the case for his apostleship. For two chapters he details his divine commission, his ceaseless labors, his deep concern for the church, and his battle scars. By the time he reaches chapter 12 he's describing a heavenly vision he received. He does all of this to defend his authority as a minister of the gospel. But a shift of tone occurs in verse 7:

143

> To keep me from becoming conceited because of these surpassingly great revelations, there was given me a thorn in my flesh, a messenger of Satan, to torment me. Three times I pleaded with the Lord to take it away from me. But he said to me, "My grace is sufficient for you, for my power is made perfect in weakness" (2 Corinthians 12:7-9a).

This is the text from which Joni Eareckson Tada drew her comments in *Moody Monthly*. It should be clear that Paul's request for deliverance was refused, not because of a deficiency in his faith, but because God intended to use the malady (whatever it was) for His own glory. The gospel would be better served *with* the thorn than *without* it.

I think it's unfortunate that the rest of the apostle's comments are not as celebrated as the phrase about God's power being made perfect in weakness. God tells us a lot of things that we don't like, so we turn our backs and walk away. Paul didn't do that. Here's how he describes his reaction:

> Therefore I will boast all the more gladly about my weaknesses, so that Christ's power may rest on me. That is why, for Christ's sake, I delight in weaknesses, in insults, in hardships, in persecutions, in difficulties. For when I am weak, then I am strong (2 Corinthians 12:9b-10).

Don't skip to the "when I am weak, then I am strong" part too quickly! Linger over the preceding sentences. Paul claims that the only reason Christ's power rested on him was because he was weak. In that case, it makes perfect sense for him to "delight in weaknesses, in insults, in hardships, in persecutions, in difficulties," because those are the very things that qualify him to become a conduit of divine energy. Insult Paul? Fine! He gets power. Persecute him? Great! He gets power.

Paul didn't like thorns any more than we do, but he finally came to see that sometimes thorns can be infinitely more valuable than blossoms. The apostle was out to pop Satan's balloon, and he knew a thorn will do the trick a lot quicker than a petal. Try it if you don't believe me.

Curiouser and Curiouser

"Susan" was diagnosed with breast cancer just five days before her mom was killed in a car accident. Her anger flared at both her father—who fell asleep at the wheel to cause the crash, yet survived—and at God. She confesses to a lot of bitter questioning.

About that time Susan had joined a new church and was beginning to get her relationship with God on solid ground. She had surgery the August following the crash and the people of her church were extremely helpful. Her pastor was especially comforting—he didn't pretend to know why God allowed both catastrophes to happen almost simultaneously, but he knew God cared.

Susan joined a small group which began to have a major influence on her. She soon abandoned her childhood conviction that she must have done something sinful to deserve her circumstances. In fact, she began to believe her illness allowed her the chance to give and others to receive, for everyone to learn the nature of true community.

Several months later Susan's back began acting up. Her co-workers grew tired of hearing about it and so urged her to see a doctor. Tests showed she had developed yet another form of cancer, *multiple myoloma*. Her heart sank.

"I thought it was unfair that I had to get it again," she said. This time she lost much of her support system, since now she couldn't often get out of the house.

145

When she entered the hospital "there was a lot of talk about getting my affairs in order, that I didn't have much time left," she says. "But now my oncologist says I should be thinking about years left instead of months."

Treatment has helped strengthen her back and she's no longer as weak as she was, but could anything good come out of *this*?

Yes, according to Susan. The whole painful ordeal has made her relationship with God stronger, more realistic. She knows that, sometimes, He doesn't allow our bodies to heal, but uses the affliction to teach us—and not necessarily just the afflicted one.

"Now I stop and rely on Him to make it through every day," Susan says, and her friends agree. They find it remarkable that this is the same woman who not so long ago was skeptical that God worked in the lives of His people or that He could really, truly, love her.

And what was it that created the conditions under which this remarkable spiritual growth has occurred? Cancer. Go figure. The "thorn" in Susan's life may eventually kill her—and yet God is using it in much the same way He did with Paul's benign handicap. Not all of God's turnabouts come equipped with happy bells and whistles...and yet His hand is unmistakable all the same.

Dr. Paul Brand, a missionary doctor to India, can certify such a diagnosis. His Indian friend and patient Ramaswamy was "ugly" on the physical level due to the devastating effects of leprosy on his body. His condition was beyond surgical help.

Ramaswamy had no ability to earn a living and had accepted the status of a beggar. "He had the downcast eyes and the whining voice of the beggar caste," writes Brand. "He was worthless to society, and felt worthless in his own eyes."[13] But that conviction was about to change in a flash of divine turnabout:

> He came to our New Life center originally to learn a trade, but it turned out that his hands were so stiff and clenched that he could not hold tools. We could not help him. However, during his stay he came to know Jesus Christ. He was baptized and took the name Paul. His whole attitude changed. He started holding up his head, and smiling. We found that he was a quick learner and a good teacher. He began teaching some of the younger patients how to take care of their hands, using his own bad hands as examples of what might happen if they did not follow his advice.

Medical students often visited our Center in groups to learn about leprosy, and we soon began to use Paul as a teacher of principles of rehabilitation. He also took visitors around, and all commented on the joy in his face. He loved to talk about Jesus. In 1991 at the annual prize-giving of the medical college, the principal of the college presented Paul with a certificate which identified him as THE TEACHER OF THE YEAR. The senior medical students had voted this honor for him. Paul's body had been a failure. His psyche had accepted defeat. Jesus Christ took hold of his spirit, and used it to restore and enliven his mind, so that his physical limitations became of no significance. Not only was he a good teacher, the students voted him the BEST.[14]

Is That a Thorn in Your Foot?

Some turnabouts are easier to take than others, aren't they? If someone were to walk up to me and ask, "Steve, do you delight in weaknesses, in insults, in hardships, in persecutions, in difficulties? Because, you know, only when you're weak will you be strong," I might very well respond with a kick to the kneecap and a "Well, brother, as you can see, I am better at giving them than taking them. By the way, do *you* feel stronger now?"

None of us likes to think about the "thorns" that may invade our lives. And I believe this aversion is normal and even healthy. I have yet to find a biblical text that tells me to pray for thorns.

Thorns come into our lives unbidden, however. We don't have to ask for them! And when we request that they be taken away, the answer is sometimes no.

It's exactly at that point that the apostle's teaching is meant for us. Learn it now; apply it then. But don't buzz around foisting your biblical sagacity on everyone in sight. Few things are as obnoxious as someone with steel-toed boots lecturing a bare-footed thorn-bearer that he really ought to thank God for the blood soaking the ground.

Even so, turnabout is God's play, even in the arena of illness and natural disasters. It is that biblical conviction that can sustain you when you find yourself in the middle of an earthly calamity or a dreaded illness. God has not lost control! His power and wisdom are so immense that He can even use Satan's worst afflictions to bring Himself glory. Most of the time He gets that glory through you.

Last Sunday the church I attend held a "parent dedication" service. Six couples brought their children forward so that the church might pray for the strength, stamina, and wisdom each couple would need to rear their children in a godly home. The event proceeded as most do, with some laughter and some tears, some nervousness and some profound insights. But the usual routine was interrupted when the last of the couples presented their daughter.

148

Their one-year-old child, they explained, was deaf and partially blind because she was born with just half a brain. Neurologists said she couldn't develop mentally past one to two months of chronological age. She is fed through a tube, since she never learned to swallow. The couple has an older son (healthy) and is expecting another baby in a few months (pray for healthy). They aren't sure how far to utilize medical procedures that will keep their daughter alive.

After the situation was fully explained, the father spoke. "I have the same kind of deformity my daughter has," he said, "except mine is in my heart. Sin has affected her physically—my problem is spiritual."

Then he stopped to collect himself and describe the work of a turnabout-creating God. No, his daughter wasn't miraculously healed on the platform and, no, his whole extended family, neighborhood, city, county, and state hadn't come to faith because of the tragedy.

"But one good thing has come out of all this," he said while we all wiped away tears. "My wife and I have grown much closer together. I've grown a lot closer to God and have learned to depend upon Him completely."

Then this courageous couple turned around and joined the other parents behind the pulpit, waiting to be prayed for by the church. Believe me, the church prayed. And I know to Whom we prayed.

The God of turnabouts.

Not the God of our fantasy. Not the God of never-never land. But the God Who knows how to turn even the most heart-wrenching tragedies into bits of divine glory.

And as I sat in the pew, I thought, *even this qualifies.*

149

Chapter 9

Screw-ups to the Glory of God

I was a high school senior and had the lead role in the intense drama, "Flowers for Algernon." I played Charlie Gordon, a pleasant but mildly retarded young man whose IQ rockets to well over 200 through an experimental surgical technique. At the height of his genius, he makes a horrible discovery: His increased intellect came only through the destruction of his brain. He learns that the more intelligent he becomes, the faster and further will be his descent back into confusion.

Toward the end of the play, Charlie sits alone in his Spartan apartment when someone knocks at the door. He doesn't want to see anyone. Although he has already started his tragic decline, he remembers his fleeting brilliance. He cannot stomach the pity. So he orders his visitor away.

It is a profound scene in an emotionally-wrenching drama.

As a captivated audience of several hundred watched, I prepared to shout out the pitiful line. I was supposed to say, "I want to be alone!" Instead, the words "I want to be by myself!" flashed through my mind. Before I could do anything about it, I heard myself screaming, *"I want to be by my alone!"*

I was horrified. The audience howled...but not, I found out later, because of my blunder. No one other than the cast knew I had mangled the line. Spectators thought it was perfectly appropriate; it illustrated Charlie's rapid deterioration, provided some much needed comic relief, and in a strange way even highlighted the greater tragedy to come.

I was saved! I screwed up, but in an unexpected way my bungling actually enhanced the performance.

Mistakes + God = Surprises

152

No doubt most of us can tell similar stories. Our mistakes, blunders, *fauxs pas,* and assorted screw-ups somehow get transformed into blessings in disguise. Probability helps to explain much of this—the sheer number of our errors guarantees that one of them, somewhere, sometime, by blind chance is going to turn out well.

Christians, however, enjoy a much livelier hope than probability can supply. Those who are members of God's family through faith in Jesus Christ can rest in the certain hope that God is an expert at taking their gaffes and using them for His glory. Our Heavenly Father delights in revealing His majesty through our mistakes.

Recently I was asked to speak at a banquet for the Albany, Oregon, Crisis Pregnancy Center. I have known for years about the invaluable work CPC does across our nation with hurting women, so I was delighted to accept the invitation. I asked a few perfunctory questions about the makeup and number of attendees, where and when the banquet was to be held, and who I might contact should I need further information. Foolishly, I didn't bother to make a few inquiries that would have greatly shaped my banquet remarks. I suppose I was just lazy.

I thought about an appropriate text for the evening and finally decided upon Galatians 6:9: "Let us not become weary in doing good, for at the proper time we will reap a harvest if we do not give up." It made perfect sense to me: people dedicated to saving the lives of unborn children are obvious targets in this society for all kinds of abuse. I reasoned that, if anyone needed encouragement to keep on "doing good," it would be the faithful workers at the Crisis Pregnancy Center. Who knows what kind of attacks they had to weather over the years? With all that in mind, I prepared my speech.

The night of the banquet arrived and I left Portland early for the two-hour drive to Albany (I often leave early because I have a tendency—more like a preordained certainty, actually—to get lost). Surprisingly, I found my target destination after stopping just once to get my bearings. I made my way to the banquet hall and soon was greeted by Patty Mahockle, the Albany CPC executive director. We chatted for a few moments when she casually dropped the bomb shell. The conversation went something like this:

"We're so glad to have you here this evening, Mr. Halliday. We're hoping that this will be a fine kick-off for the Albany CPC."

"Kick-off?" I asked, a little bewildered. "For your new fiscal year, you mean?"

"I suppose you could call it that. Actually, this is our first annual banquet. We're hoping this will give us a good

153

foundation for many years of ministry."

"Ummm, when did you actually open your doors to the public?" I was beginning to get worried.

"We hope to open our doors in a week or so."

My worry meter instantly shifted from "beginning to get" to "you are in deep yogurt." As I began to see the relevance of my talk cough, sputter, and die like a Yugo on kerosene, I managed a weak, "Ahhh, so let's see then. You, uhh, haven't opened for business yet?"

"No, that's right. But we're really excited about getting underway. Mr. Halliday, could you excuse me for a moment? I have to see to some details before we get started tonight. Excuse me."

As Patty left, I silently berated myself for not asking a few obvious questions about the Albany CPC. I had just assumed the center must have been operating for some time. It never occurred to me that this banquet would be its coming-out party.

154 But now I was stuck. There was no time to change topics or Scripture passages, so I breathed a short prayer that God would use my remarks anyway and convinced myself that if no one needed such a talk now, they would in a few months. Slight consolation, but it allowed me to go on.

Later that evening I delivered my talk and seemed to hold the audience's attention. I was hopeful that, even though the speech wasn't geared for Albany's needs, someone in the crowd would be encouraged by it. Afterward I continued to scold myself for my carelessness, but what was done was done. At least, God's Word never returns to Him void...even when it's delivered by a less-than-diligent servant.

I was unprepared for what happened next.

The chairman of the board approached me immediately following the banquet and asked if I had been told much about his organization's history. *Oh boy,* I thought, *here it comes. And you deserve it.*

"No," I said, "I can't say that I have."

"Well, that's interesting," he replied, "because your message hit the mark exactly."

Say what? I wasn't sure I had heard him correctly. "What do you mean?" I asked, more in astonishment than curiosity.

"About a month ago we discovered $5,000 had been misappropriated from our account," he replied. "And you know that these centers are run on a shoestring. It nearly did us in—we almost quit before we began.

"And then, just yesterday, we found out that our rent is going to be 50 percent higher than we had planned for. That was almost the straw that broke the camel's back. Many of us came to this banquet discouraged, really down. Your talk was just what we needed to hear. Thank you!" he wrung my hand. "Thank you *so much* for coming."

Before my head could clear, at least two other board members, as well as the director, expressed similar senti- ments. And all I could do was shake my head and point in gratitude and wonder to an astonishing God who delights in glorifying Himself even through our bungling. He's been at it for a long, long time.

A Patriarchal Pariah

It shouldn't surprise us to find several examples of this principle in the Bible. With men and women being what they are—screw-ups waiting to happen—and God being Who He is—the King of the Universe Who does all things well—we don't have to look far to see some potent illustrations.

Take Abraham, for instance. This godly man whom Isaiah calls the friend of God (Isaiah 41:8) and whom Paul

155

uses as a pre-eminent example of faith (see Romans 4), was no stranger to pratfalls and miscues. And while none of these foul-ups were good in and of themselves, God chose to use Abraham's very blunders to display His infinite glory to a watching world—and to bless Abraham in spite of himself.

The first incident is recorded in Genesis 12. Almost immediately after receiving God's promise of blessing and taking his first step of faith by following the Lord's command to leave Ur, Abraham (then Abram) trips on his unbelief in Egypt and falls square on his nose.

Abram knew that his wife, Sarai, was beautiful. He also knew that the Egyptians recognized a pretty face when they saw one and that they saw no problem with eliminating foreign husbands should the need arise. So Abram asked Sarai to lie for him. "Say you are my sister," he said, "so that I will be treated well for your sake and my life will be spared because of you" (Genesis 12:13).

Sarai did so, and soon Pharaoh himself heard of her beauty. He immediately took her into his own palace. He was so pleased with her that he give Abram "sheep and cattle, male and female donkeys, menservants and maidservants, and camels" (v. 16).

Meanwhile, the Lord was not pleased. He inflicted serious diseases on Pharaoh and his household…and somehow the king knew why. He summoned Abram and said, "What have you done to me?... Why didn't you tell me she was your wife? Why did you say, 'She is my sister,' so that I took her to be my wife? Now then, here is your wife. Take her and go!" (vv. 18-19). Pharaoh then "gave orders about Abram to his men, and they sent him on his way, with his wife and everything he had" (v. 20).

Did Abram commit a serious blunder? You bet. Could it have been disastrous? Without question. But God took

Abram's foolish mistake and used it not only to help make Abram wealthy, but to show a pagan king who the real King was.

We Interrupt This Program...

Now, before we go on, I need to clarify something. I want to make it plain that I'm not encouraging God's people to do stupid things so that God can have some raw material out of which to glorify Himself. There is plenty of more suitable matter in the universe for that.

But even more than that, I want to prevent anyone from using the ideas in this chapter as an excuse—or worse, as an encouragement—to willfully commit some sin in the mistaken belief that God will use that offense as a launching pad for some glorious turnabout. I am all the more eager to make this point after last night.

Just one month ago on March 25 the Portland, Oregon, area was rocked by a rare earthquake, measuring about 5.7 on the Richter scale. We Oregonians always assumed earthquakes belonged in California, not here, so the quake came as a bit of a...shock. The quake injured no one and did not cause widespread damage, but it made all of us a little edgy. Suddenly, we were not as earthquake proof as we thought.

Into this new tectonic awareness stepped John Guntner, a twenty-six-year-old street preacher and computer programmer. Guntner grabbed instant headlines in all the local media when he prophesied a 10.0 Richter quake would devastate the Portland metropolitan area and much of the Oregon coast. He said the unprecedented destruction would occur on May 3, and that it had been revealed to him by God as he read a passage of Scripture while crossing a Portland bridge. The judgment, he said, was divine retribution for the unrepentant wickedness of the city.

His "prophecy" was bad enough, but the pastoral staff
of the church Guntner attended copied and sent to more than
a thousand area churches a three-page letter Guntner had
written warning readers to take heed and leave the doomed
area. The local media, of course, had a field day. Especially
on May 4, when the prophesied quake failed to shake out.
Instead, Portland was afflicted that day with a tribulation of
a more familiar nature: a gentle, soaking rain.

To the young man's credit, Guntner took to the airwaves
two days later on a Christian radio talk-show to discuss his
fizzled prediction. He admitted he had been wrong, publicly
repented of his reckless actions, and asked the people of
Portland to forgive him. The talk-show host made it clear
that false prophecies were severely condemned by Scripture
and that Guntner had committed an "egregious error," but
asked call-in listeners to refrain from casting stones and to
welcome Guntner back to the fold.

158

So far so good. But what appalled me was the overwhelming number of callers who not only excused the
would-be prophet's behavior, but who approved of it and
even *commended* him for it. Sure, the prediction was false—
but consider all the evangelism opportunities it created!
Look at all the exposure it garnered for the Lord! Why, the
whole city was buzzing over the prediction; so what if it
turned out to be bogus? John Guntner was a hero!

I couldn't believe my ears. As I listened to caller after
caller bubble over in rapturous thanksgiving over the incident, I couldn't help but recall the apostle Paul's scorching
words in the third chapter of Romans:

> Someone might argue, "If my falsehood enhances
> God's truthfulness and so increases his glory, why
> am I still being condemned as a sinner?" Why not
> say—as we are being slanderously reported as saying

and as some claim that we say—"Let us do evil that good may result?" Their condemnation is deserved (Romans 3:7-8).

I couldn't help but remember his argument three chapters later, when he indignantly asks, "What shall we say, then? Shall we go on sinning so that grace may increase? By no means! We died to sin; how can we live in it any longer?" (Romans 6:1-2). What so many of the callers failed to understand is that God is not glorified by willful sin, no matter what "good" might eventually come out of it.

This chapter pointedly rejects the notion of committing deliberate sin so that God might have an opportunity to trot out a dazzling turnabout. This chapter gives you no encouragement to...

- abandon your family,
- have an affair (read "commit adultery"),
- cheat on your income tax,
- embezzle company funds,
- bomb an abortion clinic,
- spread malicious gossip,
- publicize an imaginary prophecy,

...or any other conscious, stiff-necked, rebellious, hardhearted, willful sin that might be named. This chapter was written to people who want to serve and obey God but who fear their mistakes or (repented-of) sins disqualify them for further divine use. It was written to Christians who long to be holy, but who find "the spirit is willing but the flesh is weak." It was written to all those who mean to run with the godly but occasionally trip, fall, and skin their knee.

God is not bound by our mistakes! Our very human bunglings do not disqualify us from a useful role in God's reclamation project for this old earth! Willful sinners should stop right here and chuck this book into the nearest

159

incinerator; but those who earnestly desire to serve God—but who doubt they can find work shoes to fit their feet of clay—should read on.

Now We Return to the Program in Progress

When we last saw Abram, he was just starting to recover from a bungled mess in Egypt. Our turnabout-working God used even Abram's blunder to bless him and to remind Pharaoh that God Almighty alone rules.

At just this place we come to a most remarkable discovery: *This is true even when we make the same stupid mistake more than once.* Abraham demonstrates what I mean.

The Abraham of Genesis 20 is no new believer. By then he is an old man who had walked with God for decades. And yet, long years after he left Egypt with his tail tucked between his legs, Abraham moved to a region called Gerar—and immediately reprised his lying role. Here's how the Bible puts it:

160

> There Abraham said of his wife Sarah, "She is my sister." Then Abimelech king of Gerar sent for Sarah and took her.
>
> But God came to Abimelech in a dream one night and said to him, "You are as good as dead because of the woman you have taken; she is a married woman" (Genesis 20:2-3).

A terrified Abimelech immediately pleads that he is innocent of wrongdoing, that Abraham had lied to him, and that he had not touched Sarah. Early the next morning the king summoned his advisors, told them what had happened, and soon everyone's knees were making like castanets. Finally Abraham was subpoenaed to answer the king's accusations:

"What have you done to us? How have I wronged you that you have brought such great guilt upon me and my kingdom? You have done things to me that should not be done." And Abimelech asked Abraham, "What was your reason for doing this?" (Genesis 20:9-10).

Abraham responds with the same, unbelieving rationale he trotted out in Egypt decades before. Don't miss the significance of this admission: *it's the same stupid blunder he committed many years earlier.* Except this time, he's known the Lord for a long time. He should know better. Nevertheless, instead of what we might expect—a strong rebuke—this story ends much as did the debacle along the Nile:

Then Abimelech brought sheep and cattle and male and female slaves and gave them to Abraham, and he returned Sarah his wife to him. And Abimelech said, "My land is before you; live wherever you like."

To Sarah he said, "I am giving your brother a thousand shekels of silver. This is to cover the offense against you before all who are with you; you are completely vindicated" (Genesis 20:14-16).

161

So once again Abraham ends up with great riches—and this time, he's even given the right to live wherever he pleases! This turn of events forces us to ask, Why? Why does God seem to let Abraham "get away with it" not once, but twice?

My guess is there are at least two reasons. The first pertains to Abraham. As far as we know, Abraham had no role models for his faith. His whole life was a construction site where God broke new ground. God used this man to show the world what Omnipotence could do with willing dirt (see

Psalm 103:14). Yes, Abraham failed, just as we do—we're made out of the same stuff he was. But remember that he didn't get away scott-free. Both times his lie was exposed and he was dragged before an angry king, no doubt trembling in fear. God used that fear to show Abraham that the Lord is the only One who ought to be feared (see Isaiah 8:12-14a; 51:12-16). Abraham finally learned that faith in God is much safer and more reliable than spineless lies.

The second reason pertains to Abimelech. When you consider that the word "Abimelech" is actually a title—something along the lines of "the divine king is my father"[1]—you realize that God also used Abraham's blunder to demonstrate the infinite distance between Himself and puny man, no matter how vainglorious the ruler's title. When God told Abimelech, "you are a dead man" (NASB), there was no missing this point.

Once again, God used Abraham's blundering timidity to sky-write an unmistakable message to the ancient world …and to us.

162

A First-Century Foul-Up

One man does not a pattern make. If Abraham were the only person in Scripture whose bungling was transformed by an Almighty God into an avenue of praise and blessing, this chapter might have been better left unwritten. But the fact is, God seems to specialize in just this kind of turnabout. Even in the life of someone as highly regarded as the apostle Paul.

All too often we forget that Paul was human—redeemed, yes, faithful, yes, a dynamo, certainly—but human to the core. Scripture doesn't highlight for us many of his post-salvation screw-ups. But there is one that begs for our notice.

Shortly after the Jerusalem elders endorsed Paul's preaching of the gospel, the apostle prepared to set off on another missionary journey. Barnabas, his old friend and erstwhile teacher, was set to join him. But sadly, they had a falling out—a bitter one. Let's allow Luke to tell it:

> Some time later Paul said to Barnabas, "Let us go back and visit the brothers in all the towns where we preached the word of the Lord and see how they are doing." Barnabas wanted to take John, also called Mark, with them, but Paul did not think it wise to take him, because he had deserted them in Pamphylia and had not continued with them in the work. They had such a sharp disagreement that they parted company (Acts 15:36-39a).

The root of the conflict is not difficult to identify. Paul was hard-driving, intense, razor-sharp, and mission-driven. The most important thing in the world to him was bringing glory to God by propagating the gospel. The task was central to everything he did. Barnabas, on the other hand, was easy-going, gentle, highly relational, and people-oriented. The most important thing in the world to him was bringing glory to God by helping people conform to the image of Christ. People were central to everything he did. In fact, that is why he received the name "Barnabas," which means "son of encouragement." It was Barnabas who embraced Paul and introduced him to the Jerusalem church when everyone else feared him (see Acts 9:27).

163

In other words, you'd want Paul as your professor but Barnabas as your roommate. They made a great team.

Yet here in Acts 15 we find the account of a nasty falling out between two friends. This was no cordial disagreement; it was passionate and fierce. The Greek word translated "sharp disagreement" is *paroxusmos*, from which we get our word paroxysm, which is "any sudden, violent outburst, as of action or emotion."[2]

We should not sweep this incident under the rug as if nothing unpleasant happened. Without question, sin was involved. But who sinned? Who was right? Who was wrong? Both, both, and both. In and of itself, this sorry incident was a setback for the gospel Paul loved and the church Barnabas cherished.

A "sharp disagreement" such as this one hardly follows the instructions Paul himself gave in Ephesians 4:31-32: "Get rid of all bitterness, rage and anger, brawling and slander, along with every form of malice. Be kind and compassionate to one another, forgiving each other, just as in Christ God forgave you."

But, as we said, Paul was human. So was Barnabas. And because we are dust, we sometimes treat others like dirt. This is one such example. The split-up of Paul and Barnabas cannot be considered good in and of itself.

Thank God, however, we serve the God of turnabouts! For the Lord took this ugly breakup and turned it on its head. As Luke says,

164

> Barnabas took Mark and sailed for Cyprus, but Paul chose Silas and left, commended by the brothers to the grace of the Lord (Acts 15:39b-40).

Prior to this incident there was one dynamic missionary team to spread the Good News around the Roman world; now there were two. Twice as many people would hear the gospel as would have heard it previously. Eventually the wounds opened by this disagreement would be healed (see 2 Timothy 4:11), but for now God had taken the very human failings of Paul and Barnabas and had used even them to glorify Himself. It is precisely that divine tendency that can fill us with hope today. No matter how great our failures, God is greater still!

Grounded for His Glory

Jerry White, popular author and head of the Navigators, is delighted that God specializes in using our mistakes for His glory. Many years ago he set his heart on becoming an Air Force pilot. As "a fresh-faced second lieutenant...determined to do everything right" on a crucial test in formation flying, everything went wrong:

> As we lifted off the runway, we were caught in the turbulence of the lead jet and thrown into a steep, dangerous bank. We nearly crashed. I was so shaken and tense during the rest of the flight that I flunked the test. Six days later I was out of the program.
>
> "Why?" I cried out to God. Mary, my bride of 18 months, tried to comfort me. We prayed and decided to put our future into God's hands.
>
> To our surprise I was sent to Cape Canaveral, the Air Force Missile Test Center, in Florida as a mission controller in the budding space program, and this changed the entire direction of our lives.[3]

The Whites soon concluded God wanted them to try for a teaching assignment at the U.S. Air Force Academy in Colorado Springs, Colorado, where they could reach cadets for Christ. But several obstacles stood in the way, the major one being Jerry's lack of a master's degree. He applied for admission to the appropriate program, but heard nothing. The couple continued to pray without receiving an answer.

"Then," Jerry writes, "out of the blue, I was asked to speak to a group of generals and colonels." This is what happened next:

> To prepare for the speech, I visited my headquarters in Washington, D.C. There I learned that a sergeant

165

had tossed my school application into a desk drawer. I had not served at Cape Canaveral for the required three years, so I could not attend school. A personnel officer offered to intervene. I declined, saying that as a Christian, I did not want to manipulate the system, but would leave it in God's hands.

A month later I gave my speech. Afterward a colonel said to me, "Lieutenant, if you ever want to teach at the Air Force Academy, let me know." I was dumbfounded: he was the Academy's director of personnel! Later a colonel told me I was assigned to graduate school, and subsequently I taught at the Academy for six years.[4]

A failed training flight that got him booted from pilot's school was God's chosen means to place Jerry White in the strategic position he now occupies.

The Case of the Reluctant Reindeer

166

Fortunately, it's not only big errors that God reshapes, but little ones as well. God is intensely interested in the tiniest aspects of our lives. Even those non-fatal but terminally embarrassing situations we get ourselves into on occasion qualify for His divine touch.

Several years ago I served on the volunteer staff of Son City, a youth outreach in Beaverton, Oregon. Christmas was approaching and I was to speak at one of the weekly meetings to a couple of hundred high school students. About half of these kids would be unchurched. I planned to say that Christmas was not about tinsel and elves and Santa and reindeer, but about Jesus Christ. I hoped to make the point in a fun but dramatic way.

I would be speaking from a stage while the audience would be sitting on the floor below. Our sound crew worked in a room that hugged the ceiling on the back wall, where they could control not only sound, but also spotlights, multimedia productions, and other special effects.

I had strung a wire from the sound booth to the stage below. To this wire I had attached two cardboard reindeer figures, about three feet long apiece. My plan was to begin my talk by explaining the theme, make several other comments, and partway through the speech booth personnel were to launch the two reindeer toward the stage. As the reindeer glided gracefully over the student's heads, I was going to grab an offstage shotgun loaded with blanks and blast the critters from the sky.

Anyway, that was the plan.

The crew launched the reindeer at just the right time, but the stubborn animals stalled on the wire, just out of reach of anyone in the booth. The crew started jiggling the wire—then shaking it wildly—but the reindeer refused to glide. They shook the line even harder, and the reindeer began to lurch—a foot or so at a time. Meanwhile, I was going past the time in my talk where the reindeer were supposed to appear over the student's heads. I was beginning to run out of material!

Just then some students noticed what was going on behind them and started to giggle. But I still couldn't grab the gun, since the reluctant reindeer would fall behind the major part of the crowd, and nobody would see them. So as I was stalling on the stage, my reindeer were stalling on the wire, and I began to sweat. More and more of the kids were looking up, pointing and laughing.

Finally, when I could stall no more, I snatched up the gun and shot the reindeer, the crew cut the wire, and my cardboard props fell into the crowd. It didn't go at all as planned—my graceful reindeer had become drunken, cloven-footed clowns.

I was ready to panic, but just as I was in mid-sentence, a thought occurred. What happened with the reindeer actually fit the talk much better than what I had planned. I had taken pains to point out that Christmas is about Christ, not reindeer. The reason our culture has fallen for the Santa stuff is that it's slickly packaged, gleaming, and glossy. But when you remove the slick packaging, it's really quite stupid—not unlike lurching, drunken reindeer. Who could fall in love with such a lie when you strip it of its sentimental value?

On the other hand, the Christmas story stands on its own—rough-hewn, unvarnished, smelly stable and all. It doesn't need to be slickly packaged, and in fact, it shouldn't be. Glamorizing it only helps us to miss the point. So that's what I told those suddenly very attentive students.

I couldn't help but chuckle. What I first feared might degenerate into an embarrassing disaster actually made the point better than I could have planned it. The God of turnabouts struck again! It's so wonderfully true: The Master's unlooked for blessings rain out of the sky even in the form of snockered, red-nosed reindeer!

Useful Failures

We're all sometimes tempted to think that our stumbles, foul-ups, and blunders are somehow too damaging or serious to be overcome—even by the limitless power of God. We grow doubtful that the Holy One of Israel could even stand us, let alone use us.

But when we allow ourselves to descend into that pit, we forget that our God is a God of turnabouts. He delights in taking our silliest, grandest, and even most heinous offenses and transforming them by His wisdom and might into trophies of His boundless grace. Somehow, we fail to recall His indignant questions in Isaiah 50:2:

Was my arm too short to ransom you?
Do I lack the strength to rescue you?

The answers, students, are no and no.

It's possible you may have just blown it big time. You may feel as though your blunder dooms you to a wretched, hopeless future. But if you are a Christian—if by faith you have entrusted your very soul to His tender keeping—it is impossible that any mistake, any blunder, any sin could outstrip His power to reshape it into a brilliant display of His breathtaking glory before a stunned cosmos.

Because the truth is, as Isaiah well knew, God's arms are so long and so bulging with rippling muscle that the fabric of the universe itself doesn't begin to provide enough material even for a divine warm-up jersey.

169

Chapter 10

That Was Intentional!

---

*S*eminarians often joke that their schools might better be called *cemeteries*. There's some truth to that idea.

I was in the second year of my Master of Divinity program and was up to my eyebrows in schoolwork, various jobs, and activity at church. About April I began to notice a funny sensation in my abdomen. Even though I'm prone to accidents—four broken arms, a broken thumb, a broken toe, twice a broken nose, and innumerable sprains over the years—I don't get sick very often. But the sensation didn't go away and began to get worse. My digestive system started misbehaving and I began to get worried.

I couldn't take my mind off what was happening with my body. I was almost obsessed with my fears. It was the first thing I thought of when I rolled reluctantly out of bed in the morning and the last thing I pondered before I shut out the lights at night. The school nurse couldn't offer any reasonable explanation and soon I began to descend into a depression. Within weeks I had convinced myself that I was dying.

My depression deepened over the next six months or so, plunging me into the worst season of my life. I began a round of visiting doctors, reading medical journals, and shutting myself in my room. When the school year ended, I returned to my parent's home. I imagined my body was falling apart. I started measuring my hairline to discover some tell-tale regression. I began noticing a white film on my tongue which I'd never seen. I dropped about twenty pounds and unintentionally returned to my scrawny high school weight.

My parents were astonished at my deep funk and grew increasingly alarmed. My mom, especially, expressed her worry: "Steve, we would have believed this of someone else—but not you!"

172

Despite my gloom, I still occasionally played basketball. One night when I couldn't find my athletic glasses, I angrily tore around the house shouting, "NOTHING is going right anymore! Now I can't even find my glasses!" After the spectacles surfaced moments later, I marched out the door and heard my mom breathe a relieved, "Thank you, Jesus!" Even though I was still fuming, her fervent words struck me as funny at the time. In spite of myself, I chuckled.

That was my quota of laughter for several months. I remember one wretched afternoon when I was lying on my bed, unable to understand why God would treat me like this after I had served Him faithfully. I had never gone through a period of rebellion like many of my friends had. I'd been "Mr. Clean" my whole life. Was this any way to treat a dedicated worker?

Dark thoughts about God's character flooded my mind. *What if He really isn't as good as He claims? I don't doubt His omnipotence—but what if He's really evil? What if He takes great pleasure in tormenting those who knock themselves out serving Him? What if He is an all-powerful Devil?* It went downhill from there.

You can't go very far down that road before one of two things happens: either you sink further into despair and renounce all belief in the good God of the Bible, or you recognize the absurdity of the idea and return to reality: that God is who He claims to be and that He cares more ferociously for His children than human understanding permits. *Even when it appears as if He doesn't.*

It took many weeks and a firm medical judgment that I was not about to expire before I began to emerge from my depression. But theology also played a key role: I was now more convinced than ever that the Bible is true, that God is good, that He loves His children passionately, and that nothing in the universe ever spirals out of His control.

In fact, I began to see that this wretched period in my 173 life was actually God's chosen means to move me one step closer to spiritual maturity. I had never been in any real organic danger; but I came to believe that, in God's infinite wisdom, my phantom ailments were God's gift to me so that my features might be chiseled into closer resemblance to those of His beloved Son. It was a turning point in my life.

I believe it was a divine turnabout set up by God Himself, intentional from the start.

Thus Far and No Farther

I realize that last statement may have startled you and that it requires some explanation. I intend to give you exactly that in this chapter. But it's going to be brief! There's not a lot I can say here without venturing into territory marked, "KEEP OUT!" so I'll keep my comments concise. But I think it's important that I mention one idea I haven't yet developed.

From the Bible's viewpoint, some turnabouts aren't so much the result of God bringing good out of evil as they are of God Himself arranging all the circumstances of His reversal. When you encounter this species of turnabout, you could shout, "That was intentional!" and you'd be right.

That said, there are several reasons why I don't want to spend much time on this theme. First, people attribute all sorts of things to God which He had nothing to do with. I don't want to become guilty of the same error. Still, when the Bible itself says God was behind the circumstances of some particular turnabout, we'd be less than faithful if we failed to report it. Second, a chapter like this could easily meander its way into a dense discussion of God's sovereignty, human free will, the origin and propagation of evil, and other issues tagged with names such as "supralapsarianism" and "infralapsarianism." Someone with a 16KB brain is wise if he doesn't try tackling a 900MB problem. So I won't.

174

I do think it's important, however, to note the existence of this classification of turnabout because it just might help to prevent someone from making a tragic error. When disaster strikes, some folks angrily react with one of two bitter charges against God's character: (1) He doesn't care enough to prevent the calamity; or (2) He isn't strong enough to avert it. Neither of those accusations, of course, is true, but people in pain often lash out with bitter invective. It's an unlovely part of being human.

But I wonder: would some men and women be spared from shuffling that gloomy path if they knew their difficulties might be part of God's best plan for them and not some unfortunate accident? Would it help them to remember that, sometimes, God doesn't so much reverse the Evil One's schemes as create the turnabout from start to finish?

Had I grasped this idea about ten years ago, I think I would have spared myself some real anguish.

Glory in Strange Places

Perhaps the best biblical example of an intentional, divine turnabout is found in the Gospel of John. Jesus and His disciples were walking together when they spotted a man blind from birth. The disciples immediately asked Jesus to referee a theological debate current at the time: "Rabbi, who sinned, this man or his parents, that he was born blind?" (John 9:2).

I can visualize the Lord's men nudging each other and shooting knowing looks at one another, as if to say, *"Now* we'll get this thing settled. Now we'll find out what's what. Listen up, guys."

The disciples naturally expected Jesus to come down on one side or another of the question. But as He did so fre- 175 quently, the Master surprised them by dismissing both options. Just when we humans think we have narrowed the choices to A and B, God selects Z:

"Neither this man nor his parents sinned," said Jesus, "but this happened so that the work of God might be displayed in his life" (John 9:3).

The man wasn't born blind because of *his* sin. He wasn't sightless because of his *parents'* sin. According to Jesus, the only explanation for his useless eyes was "that the work of God might be displayed in his life"!

There's no mistaking His meaning; the Greek text underlying this translation couldn't be any clearer. In grammatical terms, Jesus uses a purpose clause expressed by the word *him* coupled with a verb in the subjunctive mood. Of the six possible ways to express purpose in Greek, this is the most common. Jesus means that the man was born blind *in order that* the work of God might be displayed in his life.

Now, if the story stopped here, it would be hard to know what the Lord was driving at. But the story doesn't stop here. Jesus intended to couple His assertion about the man with a dramatic action of His own. He did not want anyone to miss the significance of the event. Jesus continued His instruction in verse 4:

> "As long as it is day, we must do the work of him who sent me. Night is coming, when no one can work. *While I am in the world, I am the light of the world.*"

> *Having said this*, he spit on the ground, made some mud with the saliva, and put it on the man's eyes. "Go," he told him, "wash in the Pool of Siloam" (this word means Sent). So the man went and washed, and came home seeing (John 9:4-7, italics mine).

176

The blind man's healing was not for his benefit alone; God had divinely arranged the circumstances of his life to accomplish something of infinitely greater importance. God used this miraculous turnabout to demonstrate several crucial truths:

1. God's power is greater than any of our misfortunes; even a man born blind can receive sight when God gives the order.

2. God is the potter, we are the clay; He has the right to shape our circumstances however He pleases for His good purposes (see Isaiah 45:9-10; Romans 9:19-24).

3. God often connects His work in our lives with some physical reminder of that work. Jesus *sent* the blind man to

a pool whose name means *sent*; ever afterward, the pool itself would remind him both of God's great mercy and how he found that mercy.

4. Jesus was a unique vessel through Whom God displayed His dazzling glory.

5. Jesus proved Himself to be the Messiah by coupling His claim to be the Light of the World with His giving light to the eyes of the blind man (see Isaiah 9:1-2; Isaiah 61:1-2).

This incident shows as clearly as any in the Bible that God is not primarily concerned with our comfort or our prosperity. The most comfortable and prosperous people in the world often have no interest in God and His glory. But to the believer, God's glory is the most precious commodity in the universe. That's another way of saying that *God Himself* is our ultimate treasure: His power, His holiness, His love, His justice and promises and intellect and faithfulness and mercy and grace and truth, all combine into infinite perfection to proclaim His unsurpassed glory and worth.

That was the point Jesus made about the blind man in John 9. It's not that God was callous toward the man's handicap or unfeeling toward his long years of hardship. But in the end, whatever discomfort (or even horror!) we believers suffer in this life is as nothing if only our lives point others to God as the greatest of all treasures. That's what the apostle Paul meant when he wrote:

177

> I consider that our present sufferings are not worth comparing with the glory that will be revealed in us (Romans 8:18).

And it's part of what he meant when he wrote in the next chapter,

> What if God, choosing to show his wrath and make his power known, bore with great patience the objects of his wrath—prepared for destruction? What

if he did this to make the riches of his glory known to the objects of his mercy, whom he prepared in advance for glory…? (Romans 9:22-23).

But I can see we're starting to career into territory I don't care to scout out just now. I do want to emphasize, however, that it is neither unloving nor out of character for God to arrange the circumstances of our lives—even the hard circumstances—in order to show the world what a glorious God He is.

God Himself sometimes picks out every color in the canvas of our lives, precisely so He can later add a pinch of blue and a swath of dazzling white—thus transforming a drab portrait into one brimming with life and laughter.

He is the God of turnabouts. And sometimes, those turnabouts are positively intentional.

The Communist and the Theologian

Just recently I read of an incident which I'd bet is an example of God at work not only transforming evil into good, but arranging the whole scenario.

James E. Mugg is regional director for Biblical Education by Extension in the Ukraine and Moldova. Several months ago Mugg was invited to the Ukrainian city of Kharkov to lead a class on the New Testament books of Romans and Galatians. The discussion soon turned to the issue of legalism. When Mugg challenged his students to identify examples of legalism in their own church, his interpreter, Peter, interrupted.

"For many years I have been put off by the Christians," he said. "I don't understand their strange customs. Why do they refuse to wear earrings and makeup? Why do they follow such an unusual dress code? Why do the men and women sit on opposite sides of the church?" He listed many such objections.

"Peter," Mugg replied, "don't ask me. Ask them! Tell them exactly what you told me." What followed, Mugg said, "was one of the best discussions of legalism I have ever witnessed," and several people thanked him for the seminar after it was over. "You don't need to thank me," Mugg replied. "I didn't arrange this meeting." Mugg never would have dreamed of asking a Communist to teach a class about legalism.[1]

Oops. I beg your pardon! Did I forget to mention that Peter was the leader of the Communist Party in Kharkov? He knew nothing of the Bible and had never entered the church where the study was being held. Yet, he had been asked to serve as Mugg's translator for the evening. Peter was an English professor from the local university.

Despite their radically different philosophies of life, these two men struck up an immediate friendship. Over the next several days they spent a good deal of time together. Peter served as translator for several more sessions and Mugg even visited Peter's apartment and met his wife. But while Peter was interested in the Bible, he was not yet ready to commit his life to a man who died on a cross two thousand years ago.

179

Finally, after a profitable stay in Kharkov, it was time for Mugg and his fellow teachers to move on to Donetsk. At the last moment they discovered the government travel agency had botched their schedule. Instead of leaving Kharkov by overnight train on Saturday night, the four teachers were "mysteriously" delayed twenty-four hours. Mugg continues:

> I was upset. Now we would miss the Sunday afternoon students waiting for us in Donetsk. Intourist assured us that the Saturday night train was full.
>
> In prayer we committed the problem to the Lord. I confess I lacked the faith to believe a solution would

be found. But on Saturday afternoon, as we wrapped up the last of our meetings with the four Kharkov groups, one of the students approached me with a paper in his hand. "Here are two tickets for tonight's train to Donetsk."

"Who told you we needed tickets?" I asked. He merely shrugged and replied with a sheepish grin, "I just thought you might be able to use them."[2]

Two of the teachers went ahead while Mugg and another colleague stayed behind to preach Sunday in some Kharkov area churches. Mugg invited several of his interpreter friends to church, including Peter. He hoped and prayed that this irritating delay in Kharkov might give Peter one last chance to come to faith in Christ. That Sunday when Mugg read the words of Isaiah 55:6-13 to the church, he spotted Peter and aimed the text right at him: "Seek the LORD while he may be found; call on him while he is near."

180

Peter did not respond to the invitation at the end of the service, but Mugg found him in tears immediately afterward. "I am crying and cannot stop, and I don't know why," Peter said. "I should have come tonight. I should have come."[3]

But when God sends out an invitation, it isn't necessarily recalled when the church service concludes. It wasn't in Peter's case. In a side room of the church that night, Peter committed his life to Christ in simple faith. And the divine turnabout was complete.

What originally seemed to be some mischief of the Devil in sending a Communist to translate a Bible study, in the end turned into a cause for angelic rejoicing (see Luke 15:10).

But somehow, I doubt the Devil had much to do with this one. All the fingerprints look suspiciously like God's.

Remember John 9 when strange circumstances or inexplicable calamities invade *your* life. And then do something else: dust for prints. You may just find that *your* Intruder calls heaven His home and lays claim to earth as His footstool (see Isaiah 66:1).

Chapter 11

Why Turnabouts?

All of us have probably been roused from the dinner table or interrupted in the shower by the insistent ringing of the telephone. That's bad enough. It only gets worse when you discover that you've left your plate of steaming lasagna or hastened out of the shower clothed in an inadequate towel only to discover that you have had been so rudely summoned by a *telephone solicitor*.

These earnest sales people want to convince you to avail yourself of a dizzying array of products and services, ranging from vinyl siding to limited-time, better-hurry offers on carpet cleaning, to space-age break-throughs in the field of potato-peeling technology.

Perhaps it's wrong of me, but I generally don't allow solicitors to finish their spiels. As soon as I know it's a sales pitch, I politely inform them I'm not interested and terminate the call. My conversations with these folks rarely last more than ten seconds.

No doubt most of these solicitors are honest, hardworking folks trying to sell helpful commodities. But I just don't buy things that way. Thousands of people must, however, because the calls keep coming. And unfortunately, some of those calls don't come from reputable business people, but scam artists.

Recently I watched an intriguing investigative report on the growing number of telephone scams plaguing the country. The report detailed the lack of federal regulation on telephone soliciting and how many unscrupulous operators have bilked thousands of Americans—mostly the elderly—out of millions of dollars annually.

The report focused on one operation that had been in business about two years. The camera swept the room where the operation took place, revealing banks of telephones and operators, a wall chart indicating that day's successes, and a bell that could be rung when an operator made a lucrative score.

But the camera lingered over the centerpiece of this operation: an advanced computer said to be able to make up to twelve hundred telephone solicitations a day. This represented a huge breakthrough for the crooked industry, since a greater number of calls translates into increased profits.

The report explained that when word got out about the extraordinary machine, calls from other solicitation companies began flooding in from all over the United States. How could they get their hands on this gem of technology? The computer's inventors were only too glad to arrange for on-site visits. The more interest, the better. Why not? The company certainly wasn't concerned about competition.

184

You don't have to be when you're the FBI.

The truth was, the FBI had set up a devastatingly effective sting operation designed to nab some of the worst offenders in the nation. Their whole "company" was a sham—including the whiz-bang computer. No such device existed. What crooked solicitors saw when they came to visit was a cleverly-concocted hoax.

By the end of the two-year sting, the FBI had amassed enough information to arrest many of the worst criminals it had targeted. And they did it through the very system these crooks had set up themselves. As I watched the whole operation unfold, it came to me that the FBI's sting provided a perfect modern-day illustration of Psalm 7:15-16:

> He who digs a hole and scoops it out
> > falls into the pit he has made.
> The trouble he causes recoils on himself;
> > his violence comes down on his own head.

Turning Evil Inside Out

I believe something very like this principle is behind God's dealings with Satan. The Lord consistently takes the Devil's most abominable schemes and transforms them into spectacles of God's glory. Time after time in biblical history you see this pattern. We've already looked at several examples, but there are many more:

• Pharaoh's decree to kill all Jewish boys directly resulted in the nurture, education, and training of Moses—all at the expense of the Egyptian royal household (Exodus 1).

• When the Philistines finally captured Samson, they gouged out his eyes, shackled him, threw him into prison, and rejoiced that "our god has delivered

Samson, our enemy, into our hands." But later when Samson was brought out to be mocked, the Lord gave him superhuman strength one last time so that "he killed many more when he died than while he lived" (Judges 16).

• A plot by jealous court officials managed to get Daniel tossed into a den of lions. But God kept him from harm, while the men who plotted his death were themselves later seized and thrown into the lions' den, "and before they reached the floor of the den, the lions overpowered them and crushed all their bones" (Daniel 6).

• Saul of Tarsus promoted a bloody persecution of Christians which began with the stoning of Stephen and which culminated in the scattering of the young church, many of whose members fled to Antioch. Yet a few years later God had turned this violent persecutor into a mighty apostle and sent him to Antioch to build up the church he once destroyed (Acts 7 cf. 11:19ff).

186

There is no doubt about it; turnabout is God's play. No night is too dark to hide God's floodlights of grace. But why does God follow this pattern so often? What is it about turning the Devil's most fiendish schemes inside out that gives God so much delight?

Fitting the Puzzle Together

I think the answer to this question can be found by considering several Scripture together. First, from Isaiah:

I am the LORD; that is my name!
    I will not give my glory to another

or my praise to idols (42:8).
For my own sake, for my own sake, I do this.
How can I let myself be defamed?
I will not yield my glory to another (48:11).

God is infinitely jealous for His name, His reputation, His glory. He will not permit anyone to besmirch His name or rob Him of the praise due that name. And he absolutely will not share His glory with anyone else—as if anyone else were His equal. God has no peers. He insists the world recognize that He, alone, is God. He is utterly unique. That is why He will share His glory with no one.

So much for the first piece of the puzzle. Next, consider two more passages that apply this idea that God will never share His glory with anyone:

The arrogance of man will be brought low
     and the pride of man humbled;
the LORD alone will be exalted on that day...
          (Isaiah 2:17).

God opposes the proud
but gives grace to the humble
          (1 Peter 5:5).

The question here is, "Why does God oppose the proud? What is so bad about pride? And what is so good about humility?"

I think the answer is that proud people try to buy up shares in God's glory. They attempt to pass themselves off as God's rivals. Consciously or not, they see themselves as God's peers. In their arrogance they lust for the praise that belongs to God alone. And therefore God makes it His special aim to bring them low, to humble them—to show the world He has no equals. The humble already know this. They know they are but creatures and they are happy to be so. They love to honor God as the only Majestic One—and that is why God loves to honor *them*.

So now we are close to discovering why God loves to turn Satan's schemes inside out. The final Scripture I want to consider is 1 Corinthians 1:25:

> For the foolishness of God is wiser than man's wisdom, and the weakness of God is stronger than man's strength.

Now, I admit that this text speaks of *man's* wisdom and *man's* strength, not Satan's. But surely it is true in the demonic as well as in the human realm. Who would say that Satan is in any respect stronger or wiser than God? God has no equals, no rivals, no peers. Not in the human sphere and not in the demonic.

So with this third piece of the puzzle in place, we can at last try to see why God takes such great delight in turning inside out the Devil's wicked schemes.

188   Glory! Glory! Hallelujah!

God has declared throughout Scripture that His goal is to showcase before the universe His infinite majesty and glory and power. He has no rivals; He is absolutely unique. In fact, He is committed with every ounce of His omnipotent energy to exalting His own name and humbling all pretenders. "I will not yield my glory to another." "The LORD alone will be exalted in that day." The Devil, on the other hand, has long wished to usurp God's place (Matthew 4:8-11; 2 Thessalonians 2:4; Revelation 13:4). This God can never permit.

So, what better way to humble the proud—in this case, the Devil—than to turn his own, most potent schemes against him? What better way for God to show His strength than to pit his "weakness" against Satan's "strength"…and win? How better to showcase His glory than to provide example after example that "the foolishness of God is wiser than Satan's wisdom, and the weakness of God is stronger than Satan's strength"?

It is very much like what God did to Pharaoh at the time of the Exodus. God, through Moses, demanded that Pharaoh release the Israelites. But Pharaoh refused. "Who is the LORD, that I should obey him and let Israel go?" he asked haughtily. "I do not know the LORD and I will not let Israel go" (Exodus 5:2). Ten times he was implored to release the people, and ten times he refused. To an uninformed observer, it looked as if Pharaoh was successfully thwarting God's plans. The strength of Pharaoh and the might of the Lord were pitted against each other, and it appeared as if Pharaoh were winning.

But not in the topsy-turvy world of divine turnabouts. Even Pharaoh's power was merely a tool in God's hand. This is what the Lord Himself had to say about the stubborn Egyptian king:

189

> I have raised you up for this very purpose, that I might show you my power and that my name might be proclaimed in all the earth (Exodus 9:16).

In other words, even Pharaoh's stubbornness and pride would in the end serve God's purposes. God knew beforehand that immediately after Pharaoh allowed the Israelites to go, the king would change his mind and send his army to annihilate God's people. But even *this* would play into God's hands:

> But I will gain glory for myself through Pharaoh and all his army, and the Egyptians will know that I am the Lord (Exodus 14:4).

And that is exactly what happened. The proud forces of humankind's mightiest ruler perished beneath the surging waves of an angry sea. Chariots and horses and spears and arrows were no match for a watery torrent obedient to every whisper of God's voice. If only Pharaoh had believed that turnabout is God's play! But he didn't. Unfortunately, he has a lot of company.

Don't Give Up...Look Up!

We've just spent ten chapters considering how God delights in standing the Devil's most heinous schemes on their head, transforming them into triumphs for God's people and into great glory for God Himself.

But so what? Does it make any difference to the richness of our lives? We learned along the way that no one can predict where or when or how God will unveil a turnabout; so what advantage is there in believing in the God of turnabouts? If neither Christians nor pagans can be guaranteed a smooth road ahead, what advantage, then, is there in believing in divine turnabouts?

190

To plagiarize the apostle Paul, "much in every way!"

Rather than list the incalculable advantages, however, allow me to contrast the lives of two men profiled just weeks apart in *Sports Illustrated*. I think you'll begin to see what a massive difference it can make in *your* life.

Two Lives, Two Hopes

Old-timers with the New York Jets professional football team had never seen anything like it. As 1992 drew to a close, the organization's telephone system groaned under an onslaught of calls. One caller after another lit up the switchboard, asking the same thing:

What could they do for Dennis?

The Dennis in question was Dennis Byrd, a twenty-six-year-old defensive end for the Jets. Make that, "former" defensive end. Even as the calls flooded in, Dennis was lying in Lenox Hill Hospital in New York City, partially paralyzed in a collision with teammate Scott Mersereau during a November 29 game against the Kansas City Chiefs.

"Maybe the fallen Byrd captured many hearts because of his matinee-idol looks," wrote *Sports Illustrated.* "Or because people felt awful that another football player had been paralyzed. Or maybe it was something Byrd said when he was praying with some friends in his hospital room the night before he underwent a seven-hour operation to clear debris from his injured spinal column and stabilize his spine. 'God, I know you did this for a reason,' Byrd said. 'I'm your messenger.' Or maybe it was the message that Byrd's wife, Angela, sent by way of Jet kicker and family friend Cary Blanchard to the huge press contingent waiting for word, any word, on Dennis's condition. 'Tell them Dennis says he's glad God chose him for this, because he has the strength to handle it,' she said. 'And tell them I'm glad God chose me as Dennis's partner.' "[1]

191

When Dennis wasn't on the field, it was a good bet you'd find him either with his family or with one of the many charities he supported. Byrd spearheaded a drive to establish a $15,000 scholarship fund to help needy children pay for tuition at a Bronx parochial school (in two years, sixty-five families have been helped); he donated time and money to Forward Face, a charity for those with craniofacial disorders; he often assisted Survivors of the Shield, a New York charity for families of police officers killed or seriously hurt in action; he supported the Helen Keller Services for the Blind. In fact, the only time Byrd was unable to oblige a request to help a charity was when he promised his two-year-old daughter, Ashtin, that he would take her to the Ice Capades.[2]

Even while being transported to the hospital after his crippling injury, Byrd showed where his heart lay. Without tears he told his wife Angela that he knew he would never again play football; all he wanted to do, he said, was to be able to hold his girls. "We'll hold you," Angela replied.[3]

Marvin Washington, Byrd's roommate on away games, confirmed Byrd's wholehearted commitment to his family:

> He's the real deal, man. The genuine article. Other guys talk about doing things for their family, but when you're around them, you can tell that's just words. Dennis lives it. He lives for his family.[4]

Such commitment to family and the disadvantaged made a big impression on the whole team. For the remainder of the season, every Jet helmet was adorned with a decal of Byrd's number 90 laid over an icthus, the ancient symbol of Christianity.

192

It is Byrd's faith that guided him before the accident and which sustains him now. It is a faith full of the turnabout power of God. "Many times when his family, teammates, and coaches have visited Byrd in the hospital," said the article, "they have come away feeling as if *their* spirits had been lifted. 'We go in there wanting to help him,' says Blanchard, 'and he ends up helping us more.' "

I said that Byrd's strength and hope come from an unshakable belief in the God of turnabouts, but don't take my word for it. I've never met the man. But writer Peter King has:

> Byrd says he has drawn strength from the Biblical verse, written in black marker on white cardboard, that is hanging from the ceiling of his room at Lenox

Hill. It's the first thing he sees whenever he wakes up—Romans 8:18: "For I reckon that the sufferings of this present time are not worthy to be compared with the glory which shall be revealed in us."[5]

Friends, *that* is a man who firmly believes in the ability of God to turn sudden calamities into trophies of divine grace. He understands the agony of triumph. And his hospital room became a compelling argument for the strength and hope to be found in wholehearted devotion to the God of turnabouts. A physical turnabout is even underway: by February 1993, Dennis could walk with crutches and had been cleared by his physicians to return to his native Oklahoma, where he will be an outpatient at St. John's Medical Center in Tulsa.[6]

Let's now leave Dennis Byrd to meet another famous sport figure, profiled just a month later.

The former North Carolina State basketball coach Jim Valvano, forty-six, was perhaps best known for leading his underdog Wolfpack to victory over the University of Houston in the 1983 NCAA division I basketball finals. His verve, energy, and enthusiasm were legendary.

Less than a decade later he was fighting a different kind of opponent. He was desperately battling the cancer which was eating its way through the marrow and bone of his spine. The article detailing Valvano's fight was titled, "As Time Runs Out." It began by recalling what made Valvano so successful as a college hoops coach:

> He didn't recruit kids to his college program; he swept them there. He walked into a prospect's home, and 15 minutes later he had rearranged the living-room furniture to demonstrate a defense, had Mom overplaying the easy chair, Dad on the lamp, Junior and his sister trapping the coffee table.

Where the hell else was the kid going to go to school? In the 30 games Vee coached each season, the 100 speeches he eventually gave each year, the objective was the same: to make people leap, make them laugh, make them cry, make them dream, to move people. "Alive!" he would say. "That's what makes me feel alive!"[7]

Gary Smith, the article's author, then chronicled how Valvano lost his energy, his zest for living, and his hope. Smith asked:

Didn't they understand? How could Vee allow himself to hope? If Vee liked a movie, he saw it five times. If Vee liked a song, he transcribed every word, memorized it, sang it 20 times a day and talked his kids into singing it with him a half dozen more times on the way to the beach. Vee couldn't throw half or three quarters of his heart into anything; he had to throw it all. Didn't they know how dangerous it was for a man like him to throw all of his heart into a hope as slender as this? Vee was a dreamer. Vee had no life insurance. A man whose lows were as low as his highs were high couldn't hope too hard, couldn't lean too far, because the next downturn in his condition or the next darting away of his doctor's eyes could send him whirling down a shaft from which he might never escape.[8]

Valvano's illness forced him to consider how he had spent his life. He didn't like what he found. One day he found himself poring over the season statistics of Iowa State guard Justus Thigpen before a national telecast, and he said,

Justus Thigpen! Can you believe it? Who knows how much time I have left, and I've been sitting

194

here poring over Justus Thigpen's stats in the Iowa State basketball brochure. I'm sitting here reading, and I quote, that "Justus Thigpen was twice selected Big Eight Player of the Week" and that "he scored 11 points at Kansas and 17 points in ISU's overtime win on ESPN versus Colorado." What the hell am I doing? The triviality of it just clobbers me. You get this sick and you say to yourself, "Sports means nothing," and that feels terrible...I devoted my whole life to it.[9]

Valvano judged himself a terrible husband and father. He lamented that he had spent far too much time away from home—he wasn't even sure he knew his kids. For twenty-three years, he sacrificed his family at the altar of athletic success. He had a hard time believing what he'd done:

I figured I'd have 20 years in the big time, who knows, maybe win three national titles, then pack it in at 53 or 54, walk into the house one day, put on a sweater and announce: "Here I am! Ozzie Nelson's here! I'm yours!" I always saw myself as becoming the all-time-great grandfather. Leave the kids with me? No problem. Crapped his pants? Fine, I'll change him. Vomited? Wonderful, I'll clean him up. I was going to make it up to them, all the time I'd been away.... God...It sounds so silly now....

But I didn't feel guilt about it then. My thinking always was, I would make a life so exciting that my wife and kids would be thrilled just to be a part of it. But I remember one Father's Day when I happened to be home, and nobody had planned anything, nobody even mentioned it. How could they have planned anything? I'd probably never been home on

Father's Day before. I might've been in Atlanta giving a Father's Day speech or in Chicago receiving a Father of the Year award, but you can bet I wasn't at home on Father's Day. Finally I asked them what we were going to do, and my daughter Jamie said, "Dad, we spent all our lives being part of your life. When are you going to be part of ours?" It hit me like a punch in the stomach.[10]

Valvano grew more and more morose until one day he read a passage in a book by British sportswriter Brian Glanville that said, "That is why athletics are important. They demonstrate the scope of human possibility, which is unlimited. The inconceivable is conceived, and then it is accomplished."

"That's it!' cried Vee. "That's why we strive! That's the value of sports! All those games, they mean nothing—and they mean everything!" His fist clenched. He hadn't poured himself into emptiness for 23 years, he hadn't devoured Justus Thigpen's stats for nothing, he hadn't. The people who compared his upset of Houston to his fight against cancer were right!

"It's what I've got to do to stay alive," he said. "I've got to find the unlimited scope of human possibility within myself. I've got to conceive the inconceivable—then accomplish it!"[11]

And that was the slim hope to which Jim Valvano entrusted his very life. He wasn't a bad man for doing so, just one who was grasping at whatever flimsy straws he could lay hold of. And I don't tell you his story so we can all shake our heads at what a wretch he's been—all of us have done as badly, and perhaps worse. I rehearse Valvano's story

196

simply to show what a vast difference it makes whether one believes in the God of turnabouts.

You can take your choice: dab on holy water four or five times a day while making the sign of the cross and desperately hoping that your will is stronger than the cancer cells ravaging your body[12]; or wake up every day to the glorious sight of Romans 8:18, knowing that both your crippled body and your thriving soul are under the protective custody of the almighty King of the universe.

Which do you choose? It makes a world of difference.[13]

Why Should You Wait Anymore?

I beg you not to follow the pattern of one of Israel's ancient kings. His city was languishing under a long siege by the armies of Aram and his people had descended into cannibalism. As he gazed upon Samaria, his devastated capital, he cried out, "This disaster is from the LORD..." (2 Kings 6:33b).

Now, before you judge him too harshly for this part of his statement, you should know that he was *right*. His city suffered for the same reason that would condemn another metropolis in the future. Years later Jerusalem would lie in smoldering ruins, the mouths of its mothers full with the flesh of their own children, and Jeremiah would write, "The Lord is like an enemy; he has swallowed up Israel. He has swallowed up all her palaces and destroyed her strongholds. He has multiplied mourning and lamentation for the Daughter of Judah" (Lamentations 2:5). And the prophet Amos would add, "When disaster comes to a city, has not the LORD caused it?" (Amos 3:6b).

Samaria found itself in deep distress because its people had abandoned the Lord. They had gone their own way and rejected God's best plan for them. The siege was a God-appointed means of discipline and restoration. How they responded would determine their destiny.

May I break from the story for a moment? It's quite possible that you, too, find yourself in deep distress. You may not be able to understand what has happened and cannot imagine why God has allowed it. You are angry and almost ready to abandon the whole Christian experiment.

Please—don't! I would never presume to claim that your agonies result from personal sin, but I do insist that even your troubles, however severe they may be, fall within the sphere of God's providence. If through faith in the risen Christ you have become a member of God's family, nothing has touched you which has somehow escaped the Lord's attention. He is never surprised, never overwhelmed, never defeated. In fact, it may be that your troubles have entered your life for one solitary reason: that God might display His limitless glory in you through one of His unforgettable turnabouts.

That was exactly what the Lord was up to in ancient Samaria, but the king displayed his foolishness and unbelief when he blurted out the second half of his statement: "Why should I wait for the LORD any longer?"

198

If only he had read the next chapter, 2 Kings 7! He would have gaped in wonder at the turnabout waiting just around the corner.

The very evening of the king's remark, God would chase away the marauding army by placing in its ears the sounds of an (imaginary) attacking force infinitely stronger than itself. The soldiers ran in terror clear back to Aram, abandoning all their provisions, their animals, their lodging, even their weapons.

The next morning, the city feasted on the bounty of its enemies—all except for one of the king's officers, who had responded to the prophet Elisha's prediction of the turnabout by scoffing, "Look, even if the LORD should open the floodgates of the heavens, could this happen?" (2 Kings 7:2). The officer was trampled in the city gate when the starving inhabitants of Samaria rushed out in the morning to fill their bloated bellies—just as Elisha had foretold.

Come to think of it, both the officer and the king could have benefited from reading 2 Kings 7.

But, of course, that was impossible—it hadn't yet been written. To participate joyfully in God's amazing turnabout they would simply have to live by faith...*just like you and me!* I can't point to any book that details future turnabouts in your life or mine. There's no way any of us can know if one of God's turnabouts is just around the corner. But 2 Kings 7 does teach us that those who wait in hope get fed; those who scoff get trampled.

I plead with you, don't be like the king. Don't follow the example of his officer. The only safe and wise course of action is to wait in hope for God.

Don't *give* up! *Look* up! You may be just around the corner from your own turnabout. Wait for God! Believe in Him! He is the God of turnabouts!

But understand, too, that His turnabouts seldom take the shape we expect them to. They're shape-shifting critters, remember? Recently I ran across the work of a certain anonymous Confederate soldier who understood this principle well. His poem, written during the Civil War, is an outstanding example of someone who has come to base his life on the conviction that turnabout is God's play:

I asked God for strength, that I might achieve;
I was made weak, that I might learn humbly to
    obey.
I asked for health, that I might do greater things;
I was given infirmity, that I might do better things.
I asked for riches, that I might be happy;

I was given poverty, that I might be wise.
I asked for power, that I might have the praise of
    men;
I was given weakness, that I might feel the need of
    God.
I asked for all things, that I might enjoy life;
I was given life, that I might enjoy all things.
I got nothing that I asked for—
but everything I had hoped for.
Almost despite myself,
my unspoken prayers were answered.
I am among all men,
most richly blessed.

Throughout this book we have seen examples like this and have marveled at how God takes the venom of hell and transforms it into the balm of Gilead.

But there is one more example that outdoes them all. In fact, it is this very turnabout that makes all others possible. The reason you can nurture any hope at all that God will intervene in your life through a mighty turnabout hangs on this one shining example of the genre. Without it, you have no hope. With it, all things are possible.

It is *the* classic turnabout, the granddaddy, the *piece de resistance* in God's storehouse of turnabouts. I call it the ultimate turnabout. And I think it's a tremendous place to cement our conviction that turnabout is God's play.

200

Chapter 12

The Ultimate Turnabout

W ithout question, it was the worst day of golf ever played at the Tournament Players Club in Ponte Vedra, Florida.

Four men vied one muggy afternoon in 1985 for the title of "America's Worst Avid Golfer." While the event sounded like it might be a lot of fun, according to Jerry Greene of the Chicago Tribune News Service, "it was pretty grim, even to watch. Spectators had the guilty feeling of voyeurs at an auto accident."

I can see why. Statistics never tell the whole story, but in this case, they come pretty close.

On the day, 124 penalty strokes were called, 102 balls were lost in the water, and 17 shots were "whiffed." Of 72 tee shots, only seven hit the fairways, no one reached a green in regulation and no one made par on any hole. The "highlight" of the day were four bogeys.

So who qualified as America's Worst Avid Golfer? It wasn't Kelly Ireland, a trial lawyer from Tyler, Texas, who shot a 179, some 105 strokes above par. It wasn't Joel Mosser, who shot a 192, nor Jack Pulford, who carded a 208.

No, America, the Worst Avid Golfer within your fruited plains is Angelo Spagnolo, a grocery store manager from Fayette, Pennsylvania. Angelo shot a 257—a portly 185 strokes above par.

Angelo suffered his worst misfortune on the seventeenth hole, a par 3 whose pin sits on an island across 132 yards of rippling Florida water. After whacking 27 balls into the lake, Angelo finally putted across the bridge to card out at a 66...on the hole.

"I didn't want to putt like that," a chagrined Angelo later told reporters. "The hole wasn't designed for that—and I take my golf seriously. Still, if I had kept trying to pitch on, I'd probably still be out there. The worst part was, after every shot, I'd hear my son say, 'Aww, *Dad.*' It was embarrassing."

After the debacle mercifully staggered to a close, Angelo was asked why in the world he continued to play the game if he was so, well, *bad* at it.

"What would I *do* if I gave up golf?" Angelo countered. "Hey, I gave up bowling because I was really bad at bowling. Of course...I never lost three dozen bowling balls in one day."

I doubt whether anyone would question Angelo's right to the title of America's Worst Golfer. He's clearly in a league of his own. He's the worst of the worst. You might say, he's the *ultimate* bad golfer in the United States.

That word "ultimate" is an intriguing word. A strong

word. An exclusive word. An elitist word. It towers over every head in the crowd and forces all to acknowledge their puny centers of gravity. It runs faster, jumps higher, throws further, and lifts more than any would-be rival. Or, in Angelo's case, it outscores them all. It simply outstrips everyone. It's a word we should use carefully and not too often, lest we rob it of its full weight.

Angelo Spagnolo is America's *ultimate* bad avid golfer. At least, he was back in 1985. I suppose it's possible (though not very likely) that tomorrow someone could challenge Angelo to a match and *lose*. In that case, Angelo would no longer be ultimate; that newcomer would be.

That's how it is with most human "ultimates." The world lauds them with extravagant praise, enshrining them on pedestals light years above all pretenders... until next week or next month or next year, when the next ultimate hero appears on the scene. I grew up in an era when Kareem Abdul Jabbar and Julius Erving were the ultimate basketball players. But today if you raise your eyes to their pedestals, you will see players who look suspiciously like Shaquille O'Neal and Michael Jordan. And they had better enjoy the spotlight while they may! Their superstar replacements are already honing even more amazing skills on the college hardwood.

There is one "ultimate," however, that will never and can never change. I suppose you could say it is the *ultimate* ultimate. It is the ultimate turnabout, the turnabout which makes all other turnabouts possible and which forms the pattern all others follow.

I'm speaking, of course, about the resurrection of Jesus Christ from the dead.

God's *Magnum Opus*

The Resurrection is *the* classic turnabout of all time. It's the pinnacle, the *magnum opus* in God's amazing reverse-spin repertoire. If ever there were an example of the foolishness of God being wiser than Satan's wisdom and the weakness of God being stronger than Satan's strength, it is the Resurrection. For in the Resurrection, God took Satan's most crushing blow and used the blow itself to destroy the Evil One.

I've often wondered how Satan could have miscalculated so badly. Centuries before the trap was sprung, God had laid out just exactly what He planned to do in scores of Old Testament passages. We know Satan was familiar with them; didn't he use the Bible when tempting Jesus in the wilderness? How could he have blundered so terribly?

One possible answer is that although Satan possesses a formidable intellect, his evil mind shrouds from him the good purposes of God. He has no inkling of God's true desires. A being who for so long has wallowed in filth and wickedness simply cannot comprehend the intent of a mind which for eternity has known and loved only purity and righteousness and excellence. So in the end, Satan drew out his biggest revolver, pulled the trigger, gloated that he'd scored a direct hit—and discovered too late that the barrel was pointed directly at his own forehead. Not only did he preside at his own execution, *but his action directly made possible our own salvation.* Satan's worst shot is every believer's best hope!

To see how this mind-boggling turnabout worked, let's back up a moment and look a little deeper into the story. Then let's try to understand how it affects us today.

204

A Whirlwind Tour through Time

Satan, of course, knew the prophecies of a coming Messiah who would save God's people from their sin. He also knew that this One would ultimately destroy *him*—unless He could be stopped. So from the very beginning the Devil tried to derail God's promises of a divine deliverer.

One of his first schemes involved Abraham, the man through whom God promised to bless the whole world (Genesis 12-18). God said it would be through Abraham's *descendants* that the promise would be fulfilled. But Abraham was already old when the promise was given. His wife, Sarah, was barren. The text does not say so, but could it be that Satan's first tactic was to defeat the promise by withering Sarah's womb? No son, no descendants. No descendants, no Messiah. No Messiah, no threat to Satan.

But Satan likes "sure things." To hedge his bets, Lucifer incited Sarah to get Abraham to sleep with her maidservant Hagar, and so to "build a family through her" (Genesis 16:2). By this ploy the Devil hoped to short-circuit God's promise. But this had never been God's plan and God did not honor the arrangement.

In the end, neither strategy worked. Almost twenty-five years after the promise was first given—and with Abraham "as good as dead," according to the apostle Paul (Romans 4:19)—God saw to it that Sarah bore a son. With the miraculous birth of Isaac, Satan's devious assaults failed.

Hundreds of years later, he tried again. This time his plan was more violent. Exodus 1 tells how Pharaoh grew alarmed over the multiplying numbers of Jews in Egypt and how he ordered all Jewish baby boys to be killed at birth. Satan's diabolical logic was clear once more: no descendants, no Messiah. But the genocide was averted and God's promise marched on.

205

During the time of the kings of Judah, Satan honed his tactics but kept to the same murderous strategy. (Murder is always high on the list of his favorite tools.) Except for the courage of one godly woman, the royal line through whom the Messiah was to come (2 Samuel 7) would have perished:

> When Athaliah the mother of Ahaziah saw that her son was dead, she proceeded to destroy the whole royal family. But Jehosheba, the daughter of King Jehoram and sister of Ahaziah, took Joash son of Ahaziah and stole him away from among the royal princes, who were about to be murdered. She put him and his nurse in a bedroom to hide him from Athaliah; so he was not killed. He remained hidden with his nurse at the temple of the Lord for six years while Athaliah ruled the land (2 Kings 11:1-3).

Once again, God thwarted Satan's attempts to derail the Messianic promise. The Devil would make many more such attempts, but each time God confounded him.

206

Finally, the time came for Jesus the Messiah to step onto the world stage. By now Satan must have grown frantic! Even though his plan had failed miserably through the centuries, he tried it once more. Satan prompted King Herod to send soldiers to the birthplace of Jesus "to kill all the boys in Bethlehem and its vicinity who were two years old and under" (Matthew 2:16). God knew these schemes, too, and provided a way of escape. Once more Messiah was spared.

That did not stop Satan. During the years of Jesus' earthly ministry, the Devil often tried to waylay God's promise. If he could not prevent Messiah from being born, at least he could try to defeat the Son's divine mission. Several times he tried to kill Jesus before the time set by the Father (Matthew 12:14; Mark 3:6; 11:18; Luke 19:47; John 5:18; 7:25; etc.). Each time he failed, sometimes in remarkable ways:

All the people in the synagogue were furious when they heard this. They got up, drove [Jesus] out of the town, and took him to the brow of the hill on which the town was built, in order to throw him down the cliff. But he walked right through the crowd and went on his way (Luke 4:28-30).

Satan could not touch Jesus—until the time set by the Father. Finally, that time came.

After years of plotting how they might take Jesus' life, the Pharisees and Herodians and Sadducees and others got their chance and seized it like rabid jackals. As demonic hosts fueled their hatred, they arrested Jesus, tortured Him, condemned Him to death, and convinced the Romans to crucify Him. It all happened so quickly. Satan must have rejoiced (if that is possible) over what appeared to be his final victory. What he had sought to do for thousands of years at last he had accomplished. As Jesus coughed up blood and took his last few ragged breaths upon the cruel Roman cross, Satan was convinced he'd won. At last!

207

No Sominex for Satan

Still, Lucifer probably slept poorly that night. He had seen Jesus raise Lazarus from the dead, and doubts must have nagged at him that, somehow, that awful scene would be replayed in infinitely greater dimension.

Was he waiting for the "other shoe" to drop? It did. And when it did, it crushed his head.

"Take 6," a popular a cappella singing group, imagines it went something like this:

Well, the demons were planning on having a little party one night. They brought beer, Jack Daniels, and some pretzels; a little red wine and a little white.

They were celebratin' how they crucified Christ on that tree. But ol' Satan, the snake himself, wasn't so at ease.

Well, he took his crooked finger and dialed on the phone by his bed to an old faithful friend who'd know for sure. But, ol' Grave said, "Ha, the dude is dead as nails, man."

Well on Friday night they crucified the Lord at Calvary. But He said, "Don't fret, because in three days I'm gonna live again, you're gonna see." So when problems try to bury you and make it hard for you to pray, may seem like that Friday night, but Sunday's on the way.

A tranquilizer or a horror flick couldn't calm Satan's fear. Saturday night he called up Grave, scared of what he'd hear.

"Hey Grave, what's goin' on?"

"Man, you called me twice and I'll tell ya one more 'gain, Boss, that Jew's on ice."

"Man, can you remember when Lazarus was in the grave? Everything was cool, but four days later, Boom, he was raised. Now this Jesus has been more trouble than anyone has been to me, 'cause he says he'll only be there three!"

Sunday mornin' Satan woke up with a jump, ready to blow a fuse. He was shaking from the tips of his pointed ears to the toes of his pointed shoes.

He said, "Grave, is He alive? I don't want to lose my neck."

"Your evilness—you yellow-bellied fraidy-cat, runnin' from everything that barks—you used to be cool...Cool your jets, Big D—I mean, my scene is still intact. You see, that Jesus is dead forever and ain't never comin' back. So go drink up, or go shoot up, but just leave me alone."

"Oh look, oh no! Somebody's messin' with the stone!"

Well, the stone rolled away and it bounced a time or two. And an angel said, "I'm Gabriel—Who are you? If you're wondering where the Lord is at this very hour, Guess what? He's alive with resurrection power!"

On Friday night they crucified the Lord at Calvary. But He said, "Don't fret because in three days, I'm gonna live again, you're gonna see." So when problems try to bury you and make it hard for you to pray, may seem like that Friday night, but Sunday's on the way.[1]

Resurrection Sunday showcased not only the most spec-   209
tacular event in history, it also pointed up the most colossal
misjudgment in all eternity.

Preordained Is Not Trapped

The truth was, Jesus had *not* been caught up in a maelstrom of events beyond His control. Far from it! Nothing happened which had not been planned from before the foundation of the world. Peter clarified these events in a famous prayer, while John supplied the timing:

Indeed Herod and Pontius Pilate met together with the Gentiles and the people of Israel in this city to conspire against your holy servant Jesus, whom you anointed. They did what your power and will had decided beforehand should happen (Acts 4:27-28).

...the Lamb [Jesus] that was slain from the creation of the world (Revelation 13:8).

Jesus died, not because of some overpowering Satanic plot, but because that was God's chosen means by which you and I might be cleansed of our sin. He died for our sins and rose again for our justification (Romans 4:25). But not only that! And here is where God's wisdom and power—even his "foolish" wisdom and "weak" strength as displayed on the cross—are most clearly seen. For it was the Devil's biggest "victory" that made certain his final destruction. The writer of Hebrews says it like this:

Since the children have flesh and blood, [Jesus] too shared in their humanity so that by his death he might destroy him who holds the power of death—that is, the devil—and free those who all their lives were held in slavery by their fear of death (Hebrews 2:14-15).

210   What the Devil had schemed and labored to accomplish throughout human history, the Lord at last allowed him to achieve—to Satan's everlasting ruin. When Jesus rose from the grave three days after His crucifixion, the Evil One's doom was sealed forever. That is why the apostle Paul could write,

"Where, O death, is your victory?
Where, O death, is your sting?"

The sting of death is sin, and the power of sin is the law. But thanks be to God! He gives us the victory through our Lord Jesus Christ (1 Corinthians 15:55-57).

It is precisely this truth that allows us and motivates us and energizes us to go forward in the work God gives us.

Turnabout is God's play! No night is too dark to hide God's stunning glory! *The Resurrection guarantees it!* That is why you and I can move into arenas of human devastation and expect to see God work. That is why we do not despair when disasters of nature or atrocities of mankind seem to threaten God's control of this world. As members of God's family bought by the blood of Christ, we are the sons and daughters of an almighty Savior Who brings good out of evil and victory out of defeat. The Devil does not have the final say. He has already pulled the switch for his own electrocution.

Turnabout is God's play! I know this is true and you can enjoy the same confidence. You, too, can be on the side of the God who delights in turning evil into good. Through faith in Jesus Christ who died and rose again, you may know certain victory over whatever circumstances trouble and harass you.

It may be that your life is crumbling around you. That does not matter. It may be that for years you have been working for the *other* side. That does not matter, either. Or perhaps you fear that your circumstances are too dark,

211

> your dreams too shattered,
>> your outlook too hopeless,
>>> your situation too confused,
>>>> your predicament too complex
>>>>> for God to work on your behalf.

When we find ourselves in the depths of some personal agony, all we can see are the boiling, black clouds of catastrophe that rain down bolts of misery on our aching heads. All we can hear are the vicious snappings and growlings of the ravenous wolfpack nipping at our bleeding heels. All we can feel is the numbing void taking over the splintered remains of our broken heart. And all we can imagine is a bleak future devoid of anything good and filled with every-thing bad.

When that describes you, there is only one cure: Remember the resurrection! Remember the empty tomb! If God can take Satan's most devastating attack and reverse it 180 degrees, no situation is so dark or hopeless that it out-strips His power.

Not even yours.

Confident to the End

It is that confidence which prompted the writing of this book. Everything you have read hangs on the certainty that turnabout is God's play. The Resurrection is the sure guar-antee that this will always be true.

Is that your conviction? Do you rest in the assurance that, no matter how bad things may look, God is still in con-trol? More than anything else, that is what I long for you to take away from this book. It is my deep desire that you come to rest in the same confidence that comforted and ignited the apostle Paul:

> What, then, shall we say in response to this? If God is for us, who can be against us? He who did not spare his own Son, but gave him up for us all—how will he not also, along with him, graciously give us all things? (Romans 8:31-32).

That is the confidence which drives me. This is the sure hope that allows us to carry on in a hurting world. And I hope what I have written has increased your confidence that turnabout is God's play—in Bible times, in history, through-out the world...and in your own life.

Turnabout is God's play! No night is too dark! Bank on it! Jesus did, and things turned out pretty well for Him.

Epilog

Coming Attractions

*T*he best thing about some movies is the trailer.

"Trailer" is the industry term for a slick, glossy, highly entertaining slice of an upcoming film designed to pack paying customers into the theater. Trailers often feature the funniest, most explosive, or outrageous clips from yet-to-be-released movies.

Just a few months ago I saw a trailer for a film to be released around Christmas. It featured the star of the show, a zany stand-up comedian, delivering line after line of impromptu silliness. No props. No costumes. Not even any clips from the movie. Just the actor hamming it up in the middle of a wheat field. The audience howled. I've never seen a stronger reaction to any coming attraction. They clapped, they laughed uproariously, they shook the seats. At least one lady screeched through the whole trailer.

A few weeks later I went to the theater again. By this time the movie must have been nearing its final edit, because its producers replaced the original trailer with one featuring actual film clips. It was a mistake. The silence in the theater was broken only by an occasional soft laugh—more like a stifled giggle than an outright guffaw. Right then I knew the movie probably wouldn't make it.

It didn't. It received so-so ratings from the critics and never caught on at the box office. Its producers would have made a lot more money had they simply created a feature-length film of the actor "doing his thing." The original trailer was infinitely funnier than the movie it hyped.

I'm glad I didn't see that film, but I have been duped by other alluring trailers. You visit the theater in high hopes of smash-up entertainment, and you leave with only your hopes smashed. I wish I could say this turn of events is unusual, but it isn't. It happens all the time. If moviemakers knew how to make their films as exciting, funny, and beguiling as their trailers, they wouldn't have to worry about competition from cable or VCRs.

Just imagine how thrilling it would be to live in a world where the trailers, while intriguing, didn't begin to match up to the real thing. Envision a film company which without fail produced blockbuster movies as well as fabulous teasers. Then suppose that these awesome previews of coming attractions were available right now, at no charge, to anyone genuinely interested. And then...

...but no. What's the use? It couldn't be. Could it?

Well, fellow thrill seekers, I don't know for sure about the movie company, but I do know the "blockbuster" and "coming attraction" parts are absolutely true. I know from unimpeachable sources of several previews of coming attractions which, while awesome in themselves, can only *hint* at the power of the real thing. And you don't even have to visit a theater to enjoy them.

All you have to do is open your Bible.

Far more coming attractions are previewed in the Bible than I can mention here, but I want to give you at least a taste of one. I encourage you to look up several others on your own!

To this point you've already recalled several of God's historic turnabouts and have heard of many contemporary ones. But since God does not change (Malachi 3:6) and "is the same yesterday and today and forever" (Hebrews 13:8), we might have expected to find some turnabouts in the future. And what dazzlers they are!

As you read about the earth-shattering turnabouts to come, remember that God no doubt has several turnabouts in store for you, personally. Although I can't predict what they will be or describe any in the lives of your neighbors or friends, I can predict with certainty that they will happen. Remember chapter 11, "Why Turnabouts"? It's one prediction I can make without any fear of reprisal, *a la* Deuteronomy 18:20-22.

215

Awesome turnabouts are coming! Their biblical previews are breathtaking! And while I don't know for sure whether heaven makes movies, it wouldn't surprise me if it did. But regardless of the existence of a celestial film company, I do know that one day there's going to be an awards ceremony to end all award ceremonies.

The Coveted Oholiabs?

If Hollywood has its "Oscars," there's a good chance heaven has its "Oholiabs."

Both are meant to honor excellence in film making, but there are notable differences between them. Consider, for example, the origin of each award.

No Night Too Dark

The Academy of Motion Picture Arts and Sciences began awarding its gold-plated statuette in 1927, but the trophy did not receive the name "Oscar" until 1931. That year one of the trophies was shown to Mrs. Margaret Herrick, librarian of the Academy, who responded, "He reminds me of my Uncle Oscar."

I kid you not. A local newspaper columnist just happened to be within earshot of the comment and soon his readers were informed that "Employees of the Academy have affectionately dubbed their famous statuette 'Oscar.' "[1] In other words, the term is essentially meaningless. (There's a parable in there somewhere, I think.)

On the other hand, consider the "Oholiab." This name was chosen to honor all the faithful servants of God who labor for the kingdom in near anonymity. The real flesh-and-blood Oholiab was selected from among the people of ancient Israel to help with the preparation of artifacts for the wilderness tabernacle.

216   He is first mentioned in Exodus 31: 1-6. In that passage the Lord tells Moses to appoint a man named Bezalel "to make artistic designs for work in gold, silver and bronze, to cut and set stones, to work in wood, and to engage in all kinds of craftsmanship." God instructs Moses that Bezalel had been filled with His Spirit and that he had been given skill, ability, and knowledge in all kinds of crafts...and that God had appointed a certain man named Oholiab to help him out.

Oholiab is mentioned just five times in the sacred record, each time in connection with his holy work. The most detailed profile of the man is found in Exodus 38:23: "Oholiab son of Ahisamach, of the tribe of Dan—a craftsman and designer, and an embroiderer in blue, purple and scarlet yarn and fine linen."

Perhaps you can see now why heaven's award was named after this excellent man. The Oholiab represents all those throughout human history who have faithfully labored for their heavenly Master in whatever capacity or calling He has chosen for them. They're not superstars. They're not famous. They don't have fan clubs and they're not consumed with building an empire or stuffing their pockets with trinkets. What *does* consume them is faithful obedience to the God of the universe. That is why God has committed Himself to rewarding them beyond their wildest imaginings.

In other words, unlike the Oscar, the term "Oholiab" is packed with meaning. Heaven's award *means* something. Eternally.

To be sure, there are other differences. Every year when earth's Academy of Motion Picture Arts and Sciences readies itself to honor Hollywood's finest, you can bet you will hear the media use the phrase, "the coveted Oscars." But you'll never hear that phrase bandied about in heaven. The tenth commandment reads, "you shall not covet," and that includes the prized Oholiabs.

217

And unlike Hollywood's extravaganza, tickets are plentiful for heaven's version of the Academy Awards. The only requirement is that you reside inside the pearly gates. Whosoever will may come; whosoever won't may not.[2]

One last difference is also among the most intriguing. Oscar kicks up his heels every year; Oholiab has but one moment in the sun. But what a blazing, glorious moment it is!

Think of it: millions of Oholiabs are even now being stored in vast, celestial treasure houses, waiting for the glorious moment when the Lord Himself, as Master of Ceremonies, calls name upon name of His faithful children to receive their due. The apostle Paul put it like this:

For we must all appear at the judgment seat of Christ, that each one may receive what is due him for the things done while in the body, whether good or bad (2 Corinthians 5:10).

Every Oholiab is for lifetime achievement, but not every resident of heaven will get one. Some will come to the ceremonies but leave empty-handed. Oh, they'll still be glad they were able to attend, but they'll never be privileged to set one of the prized trophies on the mantle of their new mansion. It'll be too late. Whether any of us receives an Oholiab depends entirely on how we choose to live while still on earth.

That forces me to wonder; are some of us tempted to give up because we aren't blessed with the divine turnabout we think we need? Are we ready to pull ourselves out of contention for the Oholiab because our suffering and pain makes no sense to us? If so, we need to regroup and reconsider.

The more I come to understand God's ways, the more I see that it is only at this awards ceremony that we will finally learn why God allowed some catastrophes to blow into our lives. It is only as we stand before the King of the universe, Oholiab in His hand, that we will catch more than a glimmer of the immense stakes involved in our day-to-day, humdrum, sometimes painful lives. And it is only as we leave the stage, Oholiab in *our* hands, with throngs of angels and the redeemed applauding our meager efforts, that we will see the culmination of some of God's more unhurried turnabouts.

We might be tempted to ask the Emcee on that day, "Why didn't You give me some explanation of my hardships while I yet lived on earth?" But even if we are still interested in posing such a question, I think it likely that He would respond much as He did while He walked among us: "Child, I had much to tell you, but you could not bear it then."[3]

It may be that only at these ceremonies will the great saints of Hebrews 11 finally see the exclamation point placed at the end of the certificate lauding their faithfulness:

> These were all commended for their faith, yet none of them received what had been promised. God had planned something better for us so that only together with us would they be made perfect (Hebrews 11:39-40).

Perhaps Jesus implied something like this when in Luke 19:11-19 he taught that faithful service in small things would result one day in placing the rulership of many "cities" into our hands.[4] Maybe, just maybe, some of the severe training exercises arranged for us down here are not meant to teach us anything at all about life on this planet; perhaps the hard lessons will become useful only in our new, eternal occupations. We may not be running cities now, but a good mayor knows the importance of a first-rate sewage disposal system. Perhaps God thinks it best that we learn our jobs from the ground up.

219

The Oholiabs are awarded not to fast starters, but to faithful finishers. God graces us with just enough turnabouts that we continue to run the race. Turnabouts imply initial pain, but promise eventual glory. Thank God, we enjoy many turnabouts in this life; but sometimes the last lap is finished in heaven.

I suppose it's something like the carrot dangled in front of my classmates and me in our freshman year of college. A first-year journalism student, we were told, hates the rigors imposed on him by a grizzled instructor; but he praises that same professor when he cradles in his arms the Pulitzer Prize—*his* Pulitzer Prize.

Speaking of prizes, do you want an Oholiab? It'll last a lot longer than a Pulitzer and an Oscar put together and multiplied by a billion trillion times. But the only people who get them are those who entrust their lives to the God of turnabouts. Happy are they who walk hand-in-hand with the majestic Lord of the Cosmos...even when the way is hard and the longed-for turnabout unfolds only in heaven.

I'm sure the apostle Peter was looking forward to receiving his Oholiab. He also wanted his friends to enjoy the same honor. At the end of his second letter (and his life), he wrote:

> But the day of the Lord will come like a thief. The heavens will disappear with a roar; the elements will be destroyed by fire, and the earth and everything in it will be laid bare.

> Since everything will be destroyed in this way, what kind of people ought you to be? You ought to live holy and godly lives as you look forward to the day of God and speed its coming (2 Peter 3:10-12a, italics mine).

Holy and godly lives make for a prized Oholiab on the mantle of your very own heavenly mansion. They're well worth anything we're called to suffer, even a late-maturing turnabout.

So go after your Oholiab with everything that's in you! Don't let the disappointments (or the successes!) of life "down here" steal the spotlight awaiting you "up there"! And whatever you do, refuse to follow the example of one of the men often lauded for his place in history. Napoleon may be well-remembered in our text books, but he is unlikely to receive an Oholiab. Most of his exploits were aimed at achieving glory only for himself and not for the God of turnabouts. In fact, the turnabout he is most noted for is called "Waterloo," and it brought him no comfort. Napoleon chose his own route.

But at least by the end of his life he understood that godly living is an essential, that unexpected turnabouts are a divine prerogative...and that Jesus Christ is their master. Just before his death, the would-be emperor uttered this remarkable confession:

> I die before my time and my body shall be given back to the earth and devoured by worms. What an abysmal gulf between my deep miseries and the eternal Kingdom of Christ! I marvel that whereas the ambitious dreams of myself and Alexander and of Caesar should have vanished into thin air, a Judean peasant, Jesus, should be able to stretch His hands across the centuries, and control the destinies of men and nations.[5]

I marvel, too. Don't you? That Judean peasant really gets around. But what Napoleon couldn't explicitly say was that the Master controls *your* destiny, too.

The Oholiab, however, is a slightly different matter. His destiny is largely up to you. You can choose to give him a place on your heavenly mantle, or you can practice dusting the bare spot where he could have been.

My advice is, forget the Lemon Pledge.

221

Study Guide

Chapter 1: You Just Have to Laugh

For those who need turnabouts:

1. Discuss Steve's definition of the term "turnabout": "Sometimes God takes the very evil intended to destroy us and stands it on its head, so that even the evil itself works for our benefit and His glory."

   A. What does he mean? How does this work out in real life?
   B. Try to name several examples of God's turnabouts either in your life or in the lives of your family.

2. Steve writes, "I'm convinced that if you wrap your mind around [the idea of divine turnabouts], it'll change the way you live." How could this be true? In what way(s) would life change?

3. Discuss the following statement: "Anyone planning to oppose the King of the Universe should take note: When

you're dealing with the God of turnabouts, you just can't be too careful." What truth is this statement getting at? How can it give us hope in our everyday lives?

4. Steve writes that "the darker the situation, the more likely it is that God will pull His rabbit out of the hat (or better, that he will turn a wolf into a rabbit!)." Why does he think this is true? What difference does it make (A) in general and; (B) to you?

5. What did you think of the way God taught the Balangao people to pray? Do His methods frighten you or encourage you? How did Joanne Shetler feel about the way God answered her prayer? How is this story an illustration of a divine turnabout?

6. Is there any situation in your life right now that you believe requires a divine turnabout? If so, describe it. How do you pray about it? What do you do while you wait for it?

From He Who provides turnabouts:

1. Read Romans 8:28.

   A. Does Paul "guess" or "hope" that all things work for the good of God's children? Why is his word choice here important? How can he be so certain?
   B. In how many things does God work for the good of His people? Does this always "feel" like the truth" Why or why not?
   C. Note carefully how Paul describes the people who can count this verse as a promise. In what two ways does he describe them? What is significant about both these descriptions?

2. Read Philippians 1:12-28.

   A. What two unexpected blessings came from Paul's imprisonment (vv. 12-13). How do these constitute a turnabout?

B. Verses 15 through 18 further describe the kind of turn-about Paul mentioned in verses 12 and 13. What details do you learn here?

C. What was Paul's attitude about his future (v. 19). How is this a good example for us?

D. How are Paul's words in verses 20 through 26 a good illustration of what he wrote about in Romans 8:28?

E. In what way do verses 27 and 28 provide a fitting con-clusion for Paul's remarks about his imprisonment? How do they teach us a biblical way to hope for a divine turnabout?

3. Read Ephesians 3:20-21.

A. Who is the focus in this passage? Why is this important?

B. What does this verse teach us to expect? How does it encourage you in your present circumstances? How does it relate to divine turnabouts?

Chapter 2: Righteous Reversals

For those who need turnabouts:

1. Steve compares God's turnabouts to "shape shifters" as on the television show, *Star Trek*. What does he mean? How are God's turnabouts like shape-shifters?

2. How is a "Righteous Reversal" different from the kind of turnabout detailed in chapter 1? How does it help us in day-to-day living to recognize different kinds of turnabouts?

3. In what way is the story of Esther a perfect example of a Righteous Reversal? What passages in the book of Esther especially point this out?

4. Steve writes, "Sometimes, God...permits the night to grow inky black before He swallows the darkness in the sudden brilliance of a supernova." Why do you think God does this? Why wait until the last moment? Have you noticed this pattern in your own life? If so, describe some incidents which fit the pattern.

5. Which of the contemporary examples of Righteous Reversals cited in this chapter were most memorable for you? Why?

6. In what way do God's Righteous Reversals have "the bead on us"?

From He Who provides turnabouts:

1. Read Daniel 6.

   A. Describe the trap Daniel's enemies set for him. How did this prepare the way for the turnabout to come?
   B. What does the king focus on in his question in verse 20? How is this question often a focus for divine turnabouts?
   C. How does this Righteous Reversal conclude? How does it compare to Esther's experience?
   D. What does the king's decree recorded in verses 26 and 27 teach us about divine turnabouts? How is verse 26 the foundation for all divine turnabouts?

2. Read Acts 18:9-17.

   A. What was the basis for Paul's confidence in a difficult missionary territory (v. 10)? In what way can this be the same for us?
   B. Describe Paul's predicament outlined in verses 12 through 16. How does verse 17 put the capstone on this Righteous Reversal? How was it related to the Lord's promise of verses 9 and 10?

Chapter 3: Special Delivery

For those who need turnabouts:

1. Steve writes that "God's packages arrive on time—His time—but we never know when to expect them." How does this make you feel? If you did have the option of knowing when to expect such packages, what would you choose? Why?

2. In what ways have you noticed that our culture tends to "shrink" God down to our size? Name some examples.

3. If a mere human spoke the words of Psalm 50:9-12, we would say he was incredibly arrogant. Yet God is not at all arrogant when He speaks those same words. Why?

4. Psalm 135:6 says, "The LORD does whatever pleases him, in the heavens and on the earth, in the seas and all their depths." In what ways should this verse shape the way we relate to Him?

5. Steve calls Psalm 50:15 "the 1-800 number of Heaven's Special Delivery Service." What does he mean? Do you agree with him? Why or why not?

6. When was the last time a "Special Delivery" package from heaven arrived at your doorstep? Describe what happened and what you did in response.

From He Who provides turnabouts:

1. Read 2 Kings 6:8-23.

   A. In what way did Elisha need a "Special Delivery" in this passage? How did he get it? What was the result (v. 23)?

2. Read Acts 12:1-17.

   A. Describe Peter's predicament in this passage. Why did he need a "Special Delivery"? How did he get it?
   B. Would you say this "Special Delivery" was the result of the faith of the praying church? Why or why not? What significance might this have for us?

Chapter 4: The Agony of Victory

For those who need turnabouts:

1. Steve writes that "God performs some turnabouts even when He refuses to spare His people the slightest pain." How can this be? What good is a turnabout that allows us to suffer?

2. What does Steve mean by "the agony of victory"? What examples of this can you cite from your own life?

3. Comment on the Chinese woman who refused to be released from prison but instead said, "My mission is to minister the gospel to sinners. What better place for me to be?" In what way is she an example of "the agony of victory"?

4. Is it fair that God delivered Martin Luther to freedom and a long life, but John Hus to the stake? Did these men "earn" their respective fates? Explain your answer.

5. Steve writes that "while the Scriptures never lift up suffering as a biblical goal, it is a biblical given." Is this true? Explain your answer. If true, how does it relate to "the agony of victory"?

6. How was the apostle Paul's execution an example of "the agony of victory"? How could he write that the Lord would rescue him "from every evil attack"? How can this same confidence be yours?

228

7. Was this chapter any more difficult for you to accept than the others so far? Explain your answer. Did anything in the chapter help you to deal better with your own agony? If so, describe what it was and how it helped you.

From He Who provides turnabouts:

1. Read Acts 14:21-22.

A. Compare Acts 14:22 with Acts 14:19-20. How do these passages show Paul understood "the agony of victory" long before his execution?
B. Notice that the believers Paul and Barnabas addressed in Lystra and Iconium were fairly young in the faith. How does that make the statement in verse 22 so significant? Why would you tell something like this to young believers?

2. Read 2 Timothy 2:8-10; 3:10-12.

A. What gave Paul the strength to pursue his ministry, according to 2 Timothy 2:8? Why does he tell us to consciously "remember" this information?

B. What was Paul working so hard for (2:10)? What kind of "glory" was he pursuing? How does this relate to "the agony of victory"?

C. Why did Paul think it was wise to remind Timothy of what he suffered as an apostle (3:10-11)?

D. How does Paul apply the lessons of his own life to all Christians generally (3:12)? Do you like this promise? Why or why not? What relationship does it have to "the agony of victory"?

Chapter 5: Speedy Gonzales, Theologian

For those who need turnabouts:

1. Steve writes, "We delight in seeing God work fast. And the encouraging thing is, God seems to get a kick out of it, too." Why is it we like to see God work fast? Why do you suppose God chooses to bring about some of His turnabouts 229 quickly?

2. Comment on this statement: "Ah, the sweet exhilaration of serving a God who delights in full-throttle turnabouts! Almost before you have time to get worried, He zips in and exchanges gloom for glory." Has God ever acted like this in your experience? If so, describe the event(s).

3. Steve quotes the phrase from Isaiah 60:22 which says, "I am the LORD; in its time I will do this swiftly." There are three major parts to this phrase:

A. "I am the LORD"
B. "in its time"
C. "I will do this swiftly."
Discuss all three sections of the verse, explaining what each

means and why each is important. Why is it crucial to consider all three parts of the verse together, as a unit?

4. Speedy Gonzalez was used to illustrate the principle of swift divine turnabouts. What other personalities or characters can you think of that would illustrate the same thing?

5. If God has the power to pull off swift divine turnabouts whenever He chooses (and He does), then why aren't all of His turnabouts fast? Why don't they all feature the same timing?

6. Try to name several other biblical examples where God performed a turnabout quickly.

From He Who provides turnabouts:

1. Read Isaiah 40:21-24.

A. What picture of God is given in verses 21 through 23? If you had to choose one word to describe this picture, what would it be? What bearing on swift divine turnabouts does this passage have?
B. How does verse 24 picture a swift turnabout? Who is involved? What significance does this hold for you?

2. Read Luke 4:23-30.

A. Describe the situation in this passage. Who is involved? What is the danger?
B. In what way does verse 30 describe a swift turnabout? Why was a swift turnabout required?

3. Read Acts 20:7-12.

A. Describe the situation in this passage. Who is involved? What is the disaster?
B. How did God work a swift turnabout in this instance? How did His turnabout affect the people?
C. In what ways is this turnabout like the one that took place in the Solomon Islands? How was it different?

Chapter 6: Molasses Is Slow, But It's Still Sweet

For those who need turnabouts:

1. Name some possible reasons why God sometimes does a turnabout slowly rather than swiftly.

2. Comment on Steve's remark that "We get impatient when we have to wait three minutes for microwave popcorn; He's content to spend decades in conforming us to the image of Christ." Does this describe your family, friends, or yourself? If so, in what kind of circumstances? Why is this so often true?

3. Steve mentions that God made Abraham wait over two decades to give him Isaac, He allowed Israel to remain captive in Egypt for more than four hundred years, and that the church has been waiting over two thousand years for Christ to return. What was accomplished in all these periods of waiting? Why give the promise, then wait to fulfill it?

4. Answer Steve's question: "What do you do if you find yourself in a divine holding pattern? What do you do should you be caught in a long struggle between the forces of light and the forces of darkness?"

5. Comment on Steve's remark that "some of God's turnabouts are like molasses in January: they take a long time, but my, are they sweet!" In what way are they sweet? How does the "delay" actually make some of them taste sweeter?

6. If you have ever experienced one of God's "molasses-like" turnabouts, describe it. What were the circumstances? What was the outcome?

7. How do events in the former Soviet Union qualify for a long-term turnabout? How would they still qualify, even if the region begins to close down to the gospel once more?

From He Who provides turnabouts:

1. Read 2 Peter 3:3-9.

   A. Do the people described in verses 3 and 4 believe God sometimes performs slow turnabouts? How does their belief (or unbelief) translate into action?

   B. How does Peter respond to these people in verses 5 through 7? What examples does he cite? How does he use these examples to show some of God's turnabouts happen slowly?

   C. Are any of God's turnabouts "slow" from his viewpoint (vv. 8-9)? How can these verses help us to wait for our own "slow" turnabouts?

2. Read Psalm 13.

   A. Have you ever felt like the psalmist in this passage? If so, describe your situation.

   B. How can you tell the psalmist wishes to believe in "slow" turnabouts? How does he help himself to move toward this goal (vv. 5-6). Would this practice help you? Why or why not?

3. Read Romans 8:22-25.

   A. According to this passage, what "slow" turnabout is creation itself waiting for? How are you included?

   B. How does this passage describe "hope"? How does this relate to divine turnabouts?

   C. What instruction are we given in verse 25? How does this relate to divine turnabouts in general?

Chapter 7: Banana Peels Under the Oppressor's Boot

For those who need turnabouts:

1. What does Steve mean by "Road Runner theology"?

2. Discuss Hebrews 11:22. Why do you think the writer chose to honor Joseph in this way? What was he trying to accomplish?

3. How is Genesis 50:20 a classic statement of the way God reverses human evil? Does this verse give you any comfort? Explain your answer.

4. Steve writes, "Joseph's story reminds us that God still sits on the throne of the universe. It is an effortless thing for the Lord to reverse human evil." If this is true, then why does God allow human evil to occur in the first place?

5. How does the statement, "The deepest thing of all in Joseph's life was the wisdom and love of God" relate to turnabouts of human evil? How can this statement help us to persevere when we find ourselves the victim of human evil?

6. How do the Christmas lights of St. Charles, Illinois, serve as a parable to remind us of God's reversals of human evil? What contemporary illustrations help you to remember such divine turnabouts?

7. What kinds of human evil confront you directly today? Are you hoping for a divine turnabout in this area? Why or why not?

233

From He Who provides turnabouts:

1. Read Psalm 73.

A. How is the psalmist's reaction to human evil in verses 2, 3, 13, and 14 often like our own? Why do we react this way (vv. 4-12)?

B. What is the danger of focusing too long on the thoughts mentioned in verses 13 and 4 (v. 15)?

C. How did the psalmist get his thinking straightened out (vv. 16-17)? How did this cause a change in his thinking? Can it do the same for us? Explain.

D. What realization finally hit the psalmist (vv. 18-20)?

E. In what way did the psalmist change his outlook (vv. 21-28)? How do his words reflect a belief in divine turnabouts?

2. Read Genesis 50:19-20.

A. What does this passage teach about divine turnabouts of human evil?

B. Why is it significant that these words were spoken through someone with a personal history such as Joseph's?

3. Read 2 Kings 19:14-37.

A. Describe the situation outlined in this passage. Who is involved? What is the danger? Why is a divine turnabout required? Describe the turnabout that occurs.

B. What is God's reaction to the haughty words of the evil king? How does this never change when pride is concerned?

C. Verse 34 gives the bedrock reason why God performs turnabouts of human evil. What is it?

Chapter 8: Mother Nature Does Handstands

For those who need turnabouts:

1. In your opinion, which is harder to deal with: human suffering caused by natural disasters or human evil? Why?

2. What two things did the prophet Jeremiah learn about natural calamities, according to Steve? What difference did this make to his outlook on life?

3. Comment on Steve's statement that "God's purposes are always good, but they may seem severe to people accustomed to sin." Why is this true?

4. Conversions seem to be one common result of divine turnabouts in the realm of natural disasters. As Nancy Swan said of Hurricane Hugo, "We're going to be so much stronger. As [Billy Graham] said it, it's time to trust Jesus." Can you think of any examples of this in your own experience? What other kinds of turnabouts have you seen come in the wake of natural disasters?

5. In what way is a sickness responsible for giving us the book of Galatians? Do you think this is odd? Explain your answer.

6. Has a "thorn" in life ever turned out to be a "bloom" in disguise? If so, explain your situation.

7. Steve writes that "Not all of God's turnabouts come equipped with happy bells and whistles...and yet His hand is unmistakable all the same." In what ways is it unmistakable? How have you seen this hand in action? How are you hoping to see it in action?

8. What kind of turnabouts are hardest for you to take? What value do they have in your life? How would your life be the poorer without them?

From He Who provides turnabouts:

1. Read Lamentations 3:31-33, 37-38.

A. What do these verses teach us about suffering? What is the Lord's attitude toward suffering? Why is it sometimes a tool in His hands?

235

B. In what ways do these verses actually bring comfort in trying times? How can they help us to keep our balance in unsettling times?

2. Read Acts 27:13-26.

A. Describe the disaster reported in this passage. Who was involved? What happened? What was the outcome? How could this be termed a divine turnabout?

B. How did God use His servants to help accomplish this turnabout? In what way is this frequently a part of His methodology today? How do you fit in to this scenario?

3. Read Psalm 119:67-76.

A. How does this passage relate to turnabouts of natural calamities or illness? How did David come to see such calamities? Do you think this was an easy lesson? Explain.

Chapter 9: Screw-ups to the Glory of God

For those who need turnabouts:

1. Describe a time when one of your mistakes actually turned out for the good.

2. Steve writes that "Those who are members of God's family through faith in Jesus Christ can rest in the certain hope that God is an expert at taking their gaffes and using them for His glory." How is this different from a non-Christian's hope that his mistakes might somehow work out to his benefit? In which camp would you put your hope? Why?

3. How does Abraham illustrate God's ability to take our mistakes and use them for His glory? Why wasn't Abraham more severely disciplined for his errors?

4. What did Steve think was wrong with the point of view of most of the callers on the radio program? Do you agree with him? Why or why not?

5. Does the idea that God can use our mistakes for His glory give us encouragement to sin? Why or why not? What would you tell someone who planned to sin in order to test this idea?

6. Does making the same mistake more than once disqualify us from useful service to God? Explain your answer.

7. In the conflict between Paul and Barnabas, who do you think was at fault? Was there sin involved? What encouragement (if any) does this biblical story give you?

8. Are there any blunders or sins in your own life that have ever kept you from entering into fullness of life with God? If so, what did you do to get back on track—or what will you do?

From He Who provides turnabouts:

1. Read Psalm 103:1-14.

A. How is verse 2 a good place to begin thinking about turnabouts of our own mistakes?

B. How do verses 10 and 11 give us a hope that God will continue to turn about our errors and even our sins?

C. How do verses 13 and 14 help us to understand why God performs turnabouts of our gaffes? In what ways does this whole passage give us comfort when we've sinned and hope that God isn't done with us yet?

2. Read Romans 6:1-14.

A. What is the basic problem the apostle addressed in this passage? How does it relate to divine turnabouts?

B. Why is it impossible for Paul to believe that anyone would consciously commit sin in order to see God use it for His glory? How does this passage challenge you, personally?

C. What practical advice does Paul give us in verses 11 through 13? How do you practice this in real life?

3. Read 2 Corinthians 4:1,7-18

A. What view of human nature does Paul exhibit in this passage? How does this relate to divine turnabouts?

B. Our mistakes and sins can sometimes cause us to lose heart. What advice does Paul give us here for combating those feelings?

C. What final promise is given to us in verses 16 and 17?

D. What final advice is given to us in verse 18? How does this entire passage help us to deal with our own humanity?

237

Chapter 10: That Was Intentional!

For those who need turnabouts:

1. Comment on this statement: "God is who He claims to be and He cares more ferociously for His children than human understanding permits. Even when it appears as if He doesn't."

2. Steve writes, "From the Bible's viewpoint, some turnabouts aren't so much the result of God bringing good out of evil as they are of God Himself arranging all the circumstances of His reversal." Do you think God sometimes acts in this way? Why or why not?

3. Steve claims that when disaster strikes, many people react in one of two ways:

A. They believe God doesn't care enough to prevent the calamity;
B. They believe He isn't strong enough to avert it.
Which do you believe is the more common error of these two? Which one do you think you would be more likely fall into? In what other ways do people react to disaster? How would you like to react?

4. How would you answer Steve's question, "Would some men and women be spared from shuffling that gloomy path if they knew their difficulties might be part of God's best plan for them and not some unfortunate accident?" Explain your response.

5. Do you think James Mugg's story is an example of an intentional divine turnabout? Explain your answer.

6. Can you identify any intentional divine turnabouts in your own life? If so, describe what happened. How did God use it (them)?

From He Who provides turnabouts:

1. Read John 9:1-12,35-39.

A. What mistake did the disciple make in verse 2? In what way is this a common mistake even today?
B. How does this incident demonstrate the superior value of God's glory over our own comfort? Why is this idea so hard for us to grasp (or appreciate)?
C. What does verse 35 tell you about the character of Jesus? What conscious choice did He make?

D. How does verse 39 put the capstone on this incident? How does it relate to God's glory?

2. Read John 11:1-15,38-44.

A. In what way does verse 6 strongly remind us of John 9:3? Did Jesus not care about his friend Lazarus (see v. 3)? Why did He stay two more days?

B. If the saving of Lazarus's life was not of paramount importance to Jesus, what was (vv. 14-15)? What does this tell you about Jesus' values?

C. In what way is God's glory displayed in this incident (v. 40)? How is verse 42 a reaffirmation of what was most important to Jesus?

Chapter 11: Why Turnabouts?

For those who need turnabouts:

1. How does Psalm 7:15-16 help us to understand the reason behind divine turnabouts?

2. Brainstorm for a minute or two: what further divine turnabouts can you identify that are detailed in the Bible? Do you see this as a common theme or as an unusual one? Why?

239

3. Why is God so jealous for His glory? Why won't He share it with anyone else? Doesn't this sound vain? Why is it right for God but wrong for us?

4. Why does God seem to especially despise the sin of pride? What makes it so hateful to Him? What implication does this carry for our own lives?

5. What is humility? Why is it so highly valued by God? What does a truly humble person look like?

6. What was Paul's main point in saying that the "foolishness" of God is wiser than man's wisdom, and His "weakness" is greater than man's strength? Why would this same point hold true in a comparison with Satan?

7. How do turnabouts of the Devil's schemes show most clearly God's unchallenged supremacy in the universe? In what way do God's dealings with Pharaoh illustrate this idea?

8. Answer Steve's question: "Does it make any difference to the richness of our lives whether we believe that turnabout is God's play?" Explain your answer. If the ideas in this book have made an impact in your own life, describe what that impact has been.

9. How does Steve believe the lives of Dennis Byrd and Jim Valvano demonstrate the difference between committing yourself to the God of turnabouts and not doing so?

10. Have you ever been tempted to echo the words of the king of Israel: "This disaster is from the LORD; why should I wait for the LORD any longer?" If so, what were the circumstances? What did you finally choose to do? What happened?

11. In what way does 2 King 7 encourage us to wait for God's turnabouts? What does Steve mean by "Don't give up, look up"?

12. As a group, read aloud the poem of the Confederate soldier, then discuss it.

From He Who provides turnabouts:

1. Read Isaiah 42:8; 48:9-11.

A. Compare Isaiah 42:8 with John 17:4-5. What claim was Jesus making in His prayer?
B. Remembering that Isaiah 42 is a prophecy of the coming Messiah, compare verse 8 with verses 3 and 7. How do these verses, taken together, show that God's concern for His glory is not a vain thing but a tremendously encouraging one?

C. How does Isaiah 48:9-11 teach us that the ground of our salvation is God's concern for His glory?

2. Read Isaiah 2:12-17; 1 Peter 5:5b,6.

A. What does Isaiah 2:12-17 teach us about God's attitude toward pride? How will He eventually deal with it?

B. What does Peter mean that God "opposes" the proud? What does he mean that God "gives grace" to the humble? What promise does he report in verse 6? In what way(s) can this be an enormously practical verse?

3. Read 1 Corinthians 1:25-31.

A. Why did God choose the "foolish things" of the world (v. 27)? Why did He choose the "weak things," the "lowly things," the "despised things" and the "things that are not"?

B. How do verses 25 through 28 "set up" Paul's comment of verse 29? In what way does God make sure that no one is able "to boast before him"?

C. In what way is verse 31 a good summary of the bedrock reason why God delights in turnabouts?

Chapter 12: The Ultimate Turnabout

For those who need turnabouts:

1. Identify several "ultimates" in your own experience. What does the term convey to you?

2. In what way is the resurrection of Christ the ultimate turnabout of all time? Why can't it be topped?

3. How did the resurrection "take Satan's most crushing blow and use the blow itself to destroy the evil one"?

4. Do you think Satan misunderstood what was happening at the cross? If not, why do you think he instigated the crucifixion? If so, why do you think he misunderstood it?

5. How does the resurrection "allow us and motivate us and energize us to go forward in the work God gives us"? What

"work" are you involved with?

6. Comment on Steve's conviction that "Turnabout is God's play! No night is too dark! Bank on it! Jesus did, and things turned out pretty well for Him."

From He Who provides turnabouts:

1. Read Acts 2:22-24; 4:27-28.

   A. How does Acts 2:23 prove that the crucifixion was no unfortunate accident? Why was it "impossible" for death to keep its hold on Jesus?
   B. How does Acts 4:28 reaffirm the idea that the crucifixion was no accident? Does this absolve the people listed in verse 27 of guilt? Why or why not?

2. Read Hebrews 2:14-18.

   A. According to verse 14, why did Jesus have to become a man? What was His mission?
   B. What did Jesus' death accomplish for us (v. 15)?
   C. What two reasons for Christ's death and resurrection are given in verse 17?
   D. How is verse 18 intended to give us confidence in the person and work of Jesus Christ on our behalf?

3. Read 1 Corinthians 15:55-58.

   A. If you were to answer the apostle's question in verse 55, "Where, O death, is your victory? Where, O death, is your sting?" how would you respond? Where are these things?
   B. How does the ultimate turnabout of the resurrection guarantee that our "labor in the Lord is not in vain"? How does this knowledge shape your own Christian walk? How could it?

4. Read Romans 8:31-39.

   A. How does the resurrection unequivocally prove that God is in the business of providing a parade of turnabouts for His children (verse 32)?

242

B. In what way are verses 35 through 37 another way to talk about divine turnabouts? What kind of turnabouts are most likely in view here?

C. How do verses 38 and 39 cover both our present and our future? How does the apostle intend this passage to affect our day-to-day lives?

Epilog: Coming Attractions

For those who need turnabouts:

1. Describe some of the best "trailers" you've ever seen? Were they as good as the actual picture? Better?

2. Brainstorm for a moment. Try to name at least ten "coming attractions" previewed in the Bible. Which of these mean the most to you, personally? Why?

3. What is the "awards ceremony to end all award ceremonies" that Steve mentions? What will be your connection to this ceremony? Explain your answer.

4. Why is the "Oholiab" a better name for heaven's (possible) award than "Oscar" is for Hollywood's? What is the significance of each?

243

5. What does Steve mean when he writes, "Whether any of us receives an Oholiab depends entirely on how we choose to live while still on earth"? Do you expect to "receive an Oholiab"? Why or why not? What can you do to ensure that you do receive one?

6. Comment on Steve's statement that, "Maybe, just maybe, some of the severe training exercises arranged for us down here are not meant to teach us anything at all about life on this planet; perhaps the hard lessons will become useful only in our new, eternal occupations."

7. What do you think of Steve's contention that, "Thank God, we enjoy many turnabouts in this life; but sometimes the

last lap is finished in heaven"? Do you think he's right? Explain your answer.

8. Steve writes that, "Holy and godly lives make for a prized Oholiab on the mantle of your very own heavenly mansion. They're well worth anything we're called to suffer, even a late-maturing turnabout." Would you describe your life as "holy and godly"? How far down the road are you in their pursuit? What changes (if any) do you need to make in order to secure for yourself a shiny Oholiab?

9. As a group, comment on Napoleon's words at the end of the epilog. Do his words cause you to reevaluate any priorities in your own life? If so, which priorities? What "speech" would you like to be able to give at the end of your own life?

From He Who provides turnabouts:

1. Read 2 Corinthians 5:1-10.

A. How does Paul characterize life "down here" (vv. 2-4)?

B. According to verse 5, what is one purpose for which God made us? How is the fulfillment of this purpose guaranteed?

C. Why should we make it our goal to please God by the way we live (vv. 9-10)? How many people will receive what is "due" them at the judgment seat of Christ? What does the phrase imply, "whether good or bad"? How does this judgment make you feel? Why?

2. Read Luke 19:11-27.

A. Retell this story in your own words. What characters are involved? What do they do? How does it end?

B. In what way is this story a graphic illustration of 2 Corinthians 5:10? How does it illustrate Paul's phrase, "whether good or bad"? How does this story make you feel? Why?

C. What is the overriding principle of this passage? What exhortation does it give? Should all the details of this parable be taken literally? Why or why not?

3. Read 2 Peter 3:10-15,18.

A. What "coming attraction" does this passage highlight? What is to happen?

B. How is this "coming attraction" supposed to affect the way we live today as believers (vv. 11-14)?

C. Why does the Lord wait to bring on this event, according to verse 15? What does this imply about what we ought to be doing?

D. Has this book helped you to comply with Peter's direction in verse 18? If so, how? In what way will your increased knowledge or graciousness change the way you live or interact with those around you?

Notes

Chapter 1

1. Herbert Schlossberg, *Called to Suffer, Called to Triumph* (Portland, Ore.: Multnomah Press, 1990), 151-152.

2. *Latin America Evangelist*, "Views from the Americas," No. 4, 17.

3. George Otis Jr. and the staff of the Sentinel Group, "The Holy Spirit around the World," *Charisma*, January 1993, 64.

4. Ibid.

5. Vera Mae Perkins, "How I stayed married for 40 years. Part II: For Better or Worse," *Urban Family*, Winter 1993, Vol. I, No. 4, 21.

6. Joanne Shetler with Patricia Purvis, *And the Word Came with Power* (Portland, Ore.: Multnomah Press, 1992), 17.

7. Ibid., 15.

8. Ibid., 16-17.

Chapter 2

1. George Otis Jr. and the staff of the Sentinel Group, "The Holy Spirit around the World," *Charisma*, January 1993, 22.

2. *The New Bible Commentary: Revised* (Grand Rapids, Mich.: Wm. B. Eerdmans Publishing Company, 1970), 412.

3. From a special mailing sent to seminar alumni by the Institute in Basic Life Principles, "How to Experience Instant Freedom from Fear, Anger, and Depression," 8.

4. Otis, "The Holy Spirit around the World," 36.

5. Ibid.

6. Ibid.

Chapter 3

1. *Twelve Sermons on Prayer* (Grand Rapids, Mich.: Baker Book House, 1971), 115.

2. Philip Schaff, *History of the Christian Church, Vol. VII. Modern Christianity: The German Reformation* (Grand Rapids, Mich.: Wm. B. Eerdmans Publishing Company, 1910), 290.

3. Ibid., 301.

4. Ibid., 304-305.

5. Ibid., 317.

6. Ibid., 320.

7. Ibid., 332.

8. "*Glasnost*, Yeltsin, and Billy Graham—Odd Things Are Happening in U.S.S.R." *World* , No. 6, Vol. 12, 27 July 1991, 5.

9. Bill Ritchie, *Wired to Win* (Eugene, Ore.: Harvest House Publishers, 1993).

10. George Otis Jr. and the staff of the Sentinel Group, "The Holy Spirit around the World," *Charisma*, January 1993, 22.

11. Ibid., 50.

Chapter 4

1. *Benet's Reader's Encyclopedia (Third Edition)* (New York: Harper & Row Publishers, 1987), 776.

2. Colin Duriez, *The J.R.R. Tolkien Handbook* (Grand Rapids, Mich.: Baker Book House, 1992), 65.

3. George Otis Jr. and the staff of the Sentinel Group, "The Holy Spirit around the World," *Charisma*, January 1993, 36.

4. Ibid., 38.

5. Ibid.

6. Joanne Shetler with Patricia Purvis, *And the Word Came with Power* (Portland, Ore.: Multnomah Press, 1992), 78.

7. Ibid., 78-79.

8. Ibid., 80.

9. Ibid., 102.

10. Ibid., 103.

11. Ibid., 103.

12. Elisabeth Elliot, *Through Gates of Splendor* (Wheaton, Ill.: Tyndale House Publishers, 1981), 257.

13. Ibid., 259.

14. Ibid., 268.

15. William P. Barker, *Who's Who in Church History* (Old Tappan, N.J.: Fleming H. Revell Company, 1969), 146.

16. John D. Woodbridge, *Great Leaders of the Christian Church* (Chicago: Moody Press, 1988), 184.

17. John Foxe, *Foxe's Book of Martyrs* (Springdale, PA: Whitaker House, 1981), 133.

Chapter 5

1. George Otis Jr. and the staff of the Sentinel Group, "The Holy Spirit around the World," *Charisma*, January 1993, 44.

2. Ibid., 44-46.

3. Rebecca Manley Pippert, *Out of the Saltshaker and into the World* (Downers Grove, Ill.: InterVarsity Press, 1979), 45.

4. Ibid., 46.

5. Ibid., 47.

Chapter 6

1. George Otis Jr. and the staff of the Sentinel Group, "The Holy Spirit around the World," *Charisma*, January 1993, 38-40.

2. Philip Yancey, *Praying with the KGB* (Portland, Ore.: Multnomah Press, 1992), 40.

3. Roger C. Palms, "In Russia: Something Beyond All Expectation," *Decision*, January 1993, Vol. 34, No. 1, 13.

4. Ibid., 13.

5. Major General David Robinson, "Is Anyone in Charge?" *Command*, Fall 1992, Vol. 41, No. 3, 7.

6. Ibid.

7. Yancey, *Praying,* 17.

8. "People and Events" column, "Miracle in Moscow for Billy Graham," *Charisma*, January 1993, 80.

9. "Spiritual Songs in the Army," *Decision*, January 1993, Vol. 34, No. 1, 12.

10. Palms, "In Russia," 10-11.

11. Ibid., 7.

12. Ibid., 9.

13. Yancey, *Praying,* 43.

14. Otis, "The Holy Spirit around the World," 58.

15. Palms, "In Russia," 10-11.

16. Ibid., 12.

17. Yancey, *Praying,* 9.

18. Major Yuri Belov, "United in Jesus," *Command*, Fall 1992, Vol. 41, No. 3, 12.

19. Lieutenant Colonel Mikhail Smyslov, "Baptists with Epaulets and Without," *Command*, Fall 1992, Vol. 41, No. 3, 11.

20. Ibid.

21. Ibid., 10, 11.

22. Tomas C. Oden, "Moscow State Discovers Religion," *Christianity Today*, 24 June 1991, Vol. 35, No. 7, 29.

23. Ibid.

24. Belov, "United in Jesus," 13.

25. Yancey, *Praying,* 68.

250 Chapter 7

1. "Nurnberg Rally," *The Encyclopaedia Britannica*, 15th ed., Vol. 8 (Chicago: Encyclopaedia Britannica, Inc., 1988), 833.

2. John Piper, *Desiring God* (Portland, Ore.: Multnomah Press, 1986), 26.

3. George Otis Jr. and the staff of the Sentinel Group, "The Holy Spirit around the World," *Charisma*, January 1993, 22.

4. Ibid., 22-23.

5. Ibid., 22.

6. Ibid., 21.

7. Franklin Graham, *Results for the Kingdom*, unpublished manuscript by the Samaritan's Purse, final draft August 1989, from a chapter titled "Providing a Helping Hand," no pages given.

8. Otis, "The Holy Spirit around the World," 30.

9. Ibid., 35.

Notes

Chapter 8

1. "Earthquakes," *The Encyclopaedia Britannica,* 15th ed., Vol. 17 (Chicago: Encyclopaedia Britannica, Inc., 1988), 614.
2. Ibid.
3. Samaritan's Purse newsletter, August 1990, 2-3.
4. "Graham and son aid Hugo victims," *The Christian Courier,* Vol. 14, No. 10, October 1989.
5. Elsa F. McDowell and Andy Black, "Graham comforts hurricane victims," *The Post-Courier,* 7 November 1989.
6. Ibid.
7. Ray Holder, "Holder Happenings" newsletter, June 1989.
8. Ibid.
9. Ray Holder, "Holder Happenings" newsletter, October 1992.
10. Ibid.
11. Ibid.
12. Henry Davidoff, ed., *The Pocket Book of Quotations* (New York: Pocket Books, 1952), 323.
13. Paul Brand, *The Forever Feast* (Ann Arbor, Mich.: Servant Publications, 1993), ch. 16, mss. pp. 4,5.
14. Ibid.

Chapter 9

1. *New Bible Dictionary,* 2nd ed. (Wheaton, Ill.: Tyndale House Publishers, 1982), 4.
2. *The Random House College Dictionary, Revised Edition* (New York: Random House, 1988), 968.
3. Jerry White, "Leaving It in God's Hands," *Decision,* Vol. 34, No. 1, January 1993, 32.
4. Ibid.

Chapter 10

1. James E. Mugg, "Time to Make the Cut," *Moody Monthly,* Vol. 93, No. 5, January 1993, 26.
2. Ibid., 28.
3. Ibid.

Chapter 11

1. Peter King, "He Has the Strength," *Sports Illustrated*, 14 December 1992, Vol. 77, No. 25, 22-23.

2. Ibid., 24.

3. Ibid., 27.

4. Ibid., 24.

5. Ibid., 27.

6. "New York doctors release Byrd to return to Oklahoma home," *The Oregonian*, 10 February 1993, Sec. D, 1.

7. Gary Smith, "As Time Runs Out," *Sports Illustrated*, 11 January 1993, Vol. 78, No. 1, 13.

8. Ibid., 16.

9. Ibid., 17.

10. Ibid., 18.

11. Ibid., 25.

12. Ibid., 12.

13. Cancer finally took Jim Valvano's life on April 28, 1993.

Chapter 12

1. Take 6, "Sunday's On the Way," from *So Much 2 Say* (1983, Some-O-Dat Music BMI, admin. by Dayspring Music, a Div. of Word, Inc.). Used by permission.

Epilog

1. Robert Hendrickson, *The Facts on File Encyclopedia of Word and Phrase Origins* (New York: Facts on File Publications, 1987), 395.

2. *See* Revelation 22:14-15,17.

3. *See* John 16:12.

4. *See* 2 Timothy 2:12; Revelation 5:10; 20:6; 22:5.

5. Major General David Robinson, "Is Anyone in Charge?" *Command*, Fall 1992, Vol. 41, No. 3, 7.